From Southern Wrongs to Civil Rights

From Southern Wrongs
to Civil Rights

The Memoir of a White Civil Rights Activist

SARA MITCHELL PARSONS

With a Foreword by David J. Garrow

THE UNIVERSITY OF ALABAMA PRESS
Tuscaloosa and London

1 2 3 4 5 6 7 8 9 . 08 07 06 05 04 03 02 01 00

Typeface: Perpetua

∞

The paper on which this book is printed meets the minimum requirements of American
National Standard for Information Science–Permanence of Paper for Printed Library
Materials, ANSI Z39.48-1984.

Library of Congress Cataloging-in-Publication Data

Parsons, Sara Mitchell, 1912–

From southern wrongs to civil rights : the memoir of a white civil
rights activist / Sara Mitchell Parsons ; with a foreword by David J. Garrow.

p.   cm.

ISBN 0-8173-1026-6 (alk. paper)

1. Parsons, Sara Mitchell, 1912–   2. Women civil rights
workers—Georgia—Atlanta—Biography.   3. Civil rights
workers—Georgia—Atlanta—Biography.   4. White
women—Georgia—Atlanta—Biography.   5. Afro-Americans—Civil
rights—Georgia—History—20th century.   6. Atlanta (Ga.)—Biography.
7. Atlanta (Ga.)—Race relations.   8. Atlanta (Ga.)—Politics and
government—20th century.   I. Title.

F294.A853 P37   2000

323'.092—dc21   00-008214

British Library Cataloguing-in-Publication Data available

To Tom and Perry,
Sandra and Carolyn,
and my civil rights friends
who made this book possible

In a scene from Spike Lee's movie *Malcolm X,* a young white woman comes up to Malcolm after a speech he made at Harvard and asks, "What can a decent white woman do to help your movement?"

"Nothing," Malcolm answers abruptly and walks away.

Contents

Foreword by David J. Garrow

xi

Introduction

xxiii

1. Growing Up Southern

1

2. From Buckhead to Brotherhood

14

3. Running Scared for Public Office

37

4. Crisis in the Bible Belt

53

5. "Men Don't Like Women on Boards"

73

6. Sunday Morning at Ebenezer

91

7. Not the Best of Times

100

8. From Southern Wrongs to Civil Rights

118

9. The Second Time Around

129

10. Long Journey to a New Life

141

11. The Dove Flies On

164

12. What Has Happened to the Dream?

174

Index

181

Foreword

DAVID J. GARROW

Sara Mitchell Parsons's wonderful autobiographical memoir tells at least two notably important stories. First, it describes how she, following her 1961 election to the Atlanta Board of Education, became one of the South's first white elected officials who openly advocated racial equality at a time when almost every other white public office-holder either demagogically championed racial segregation or quietly tolerated it. Second, and just as significant, it relates how both before and after her election to public office, she broke free from the deeply rooted societal expectation that a white upper-class suburban house-wife was supposed to live her life simply as a meek appendage of her husband and instead became an outspokenly independent political voice who defied and then divorced herself from the traditional gender-role strictures within which she had been raised. One can read this memoir as a poignant account of how one southern white church-goer rather quickly enlisted on behalf of black civil rights and educational equality once southern reality forced her to confront those questions. But one should also read this autobiography as an early and important feminist account of self-realization and self-development at a time when the "women's movement" had not yet joined the "civil rights movement" in America's political lexicon of the 1960s.[1]

The historical literature on white southerners who dissented from their region's racial orthodoxy prior to the mid-1960s is relatively copious and sometimes overdrawn,[2] but Sara Mitchell Parsons's here-

tofore little-known story underscores how she came to be a voice of
dissent largely on her own within the local precincts of Atlanta and
without benefit of the wider political or academic experiences that
helped radicalize other southerners who spoke out in defiance of local
conventions, such as Virginia Foster Durr,[3] J. Waties Waring,[4] Myles
Horton,[5] James A. Dombrowski,[6] and Lillian Smith.[7] Atlanta in the
1950s may have had a decidedly more moderate political climate on
issues of race than most southern cities, in part because of both longtime mayor William B. Hartsfield[8] and influential police chief Herbert T.
Jenkins,[9] but only a small number of aging politicians and local histo-
rians can readily recall how the notorious segregationist Lester Maddox[10] was the number one opponent both in Hartsfield's final 1957
reelection race and in the September 1961 run-off that vaulted Ivan
Allen, Jr., into office as Hartsfield's anointed successor.[11]

That same September 1961 run-off also marked Sara Mitchell's
election to the Atlanta school board, but—as this memoir shows—
her own evolution as a political freethinker and incipient feminist who
no longer acquiesced to her husband's old-fashioned presumption of
wifely subservience had begun several years earlier with active involvement in the League of Women Voters. A series of league experiences brought her face-to-face with racial and educational realities
that otherwise would not have penetrated the upper-class social world
of a suburban Buckhead housewife, and from there the "new" Sara's
path toward a surprising emergence as a successful political candidate
and an outspoken public figure proceeded rapidly apace. Our histori-
ography of black southern civil rights activism has (finally) come to
acknowledge and sometimes highlight the disproportionately important roles that black *women* played in many of the movement's most
crucial episodes,[12] but the more mainstream histories of the South
during those years have yet to illuminate fully the similar impact that
white female political activism on the part of women such as Sara
Mitchell, Eliza Paschall, Frances Pauley, and Helen Bullard had on cities like Atlanta.[13] Both autobiographies and a long list of broader political histories provide wide-ranging accounts of Atlanta public life in

the 1960s,[14] but none of these volumes either comprehensively or even partially surveys the extent to which women emerged as new players on the city's public stage. Existing scholarship already attests to how the involvement of younger women in "movement" organizations like the Student Nonviolent Coordinating Committee (SNCC) helped pave the way for the women's movement of the late 1960s,[15] but the ways in which the movement's presence also encouraged other women like Sara Mitchell to step forward with a new commitment to activism and self-determination have not yet been fully plumbed. *From Southern Wrongs to Civil Rights* ought to assist significantly in sparking such an appreciation.

Sara Mitchell does not appear as a major character in any of the existing historical surveys of 1960s Atlanta, but the microfilmed editions of the city's two principal daily newspapers of that decade, the *Atlanta Constitution* and the *Atlanta Journal,* are replete with stories about her vocal presence on the city's public stage. Early in her initial 1961 school board campaign against two other serious candidates, one *Constitution* editor spent an entire column telling prospective voters that Mitchell's "completely honest manner" already marked her as a most unusual political competitor, for "this kind of honesty is seldom seen." What's more, the columnist's endorsement hardly stopped there, for he also felt moved to tell readers that "you couldn't vote for a prettier politician than Sara Mitchell."[16] A personal profile authored by a female reporter one day later paid less attention to Mitchell's looks and more to her feelings about campaigning: "It's not fun but I'm not sorry."[17] After Mitchell led the field in the first primary but then faced a run-off against businessman Dan MacIntyre III,[18] the *Constitution* ran a front page, "above the fold" election day editorial endorsing both mayoral favorite Ivan Allen and Mitchell.[19] Mitchell defeated MacIntyre handily, by a margin of 54,567 to 36,127,[20] perhaps in part because of the *Constitution*'s ardent support, and even before officially taking office on January 1, 1962, Mitchell began making headlines with calls for new priorities in city schools.[21]

Once in office, Mitchell's commitment to make personal visits to each and every school in the entire system drew press attention,[22] as did her campaign to reduce the extent of resources the system devoted to high school athletics.[23] Local columnists praised her outspokenness as "courageous,"[24] but when Mitchell began publicly denouncing the system's second-class treatment of schools that were still all-black, the Atlanta newspapers accorded her comments front-page headlines.[25]

Mitchell drew even greater public attention when she extended her criticisms of white racial practices to Atlanta's churches. "They practice so many sins they can't preach the truth," and "There is no leadership when it is most needed," she told an Atlanta audience. She also emphasized that any worries about her prospects for reelection in 1965 did not enter into her thinking: "I would rather say what I want to say in four years, than stay eight or 12 years and say nothing."[26]

Mitchell's targeting of such sacred cows as high school football, segregated schools, and pusillanimous churches earned her a full-blown portrait in the joint Sunday editions of the Atlanta newspapers. "I said what I thought," Mitchell declared, explaining that she was "shocked and surprised" at how her comments about white churches looked when set down in print in the Atlanta papers. "I made no blanket indictment of churches," and no one should think she was irreligious. "If I'm rash or radical today, it is because I learned rashness and radicalism in the Methodist Church." Mitchell further acknowledged, however, that her earlier encounter with the question of whether to abolish segregation within the League of Women voters—a story she recounts in detail in this memoir—had proven especially influential: "The experience convinced me I had to take a position on real and present decisions."[27]

Mitchell's outspokenness continued apace both before and after her 1965 reelection to a second four-year term on the school board.[28] Local groups honored Mitchell for what one citation described as her belief "that every child deserves equality of educational opportunity to fulfill his fullest potential as a person and citizen,"[29] and by the mid

1960s Mitchell's interests had expanded to encompass the wider economic agenda of antipoverty initiatives.[30] Even after more than six years in office Mitchell was still publicly lambasting city school administrators as racially "paternalistic,"[31] and only her late 1968 decision to marry California-based Tom Parsons removed her from Atlanta political life and the front pages of Atlanta's newspapers.[32]

Sara Mitchell Parsons will tell you all about those rich and eventful years in this winsome and sometimes impressive story. And even today, at more than eighty-five years of age, Sara Parsons remains an undaunted and outspoken voice. As she'll recount, she and Tom returned to Atlanta in 1986 after eighteen years in northern California, and her regular letters to the editor in the Atlanta newspapers show that Sara's lost none of her spark notwithstanding the passage of three decades' time.[33] Her willingness to speak out bluntly about the obstacles thwarting high-quality public education has not changed, as one 1999 letter readily revealed:

> The current barrage of criticism of public school teachers and administrators is counterproductive and unfair. The growing problems they face in today's classrooms are overwhelming. Among them are overcrowded classrooms, understaffing, too many extracurricular activities, too little time for basic education, too many students with too much on their minds besides getting an education, and too many indifferent, uncaring parents.[34]

As you'll see, Sara Mitchell Parsons's presence has been a gift to Atlanta that should not be forgotten, just as this book is a gift to those of us who welcome a fuller understanding of how the 1960s helped liberate a wide range of Americans of all races and genders.

David J. Garrow, Presidential Distinguished Professor at Emory University School of Law, is the author of *Bearing the Cross,* a Pulitzer

Prize–winning biography of Martin Luther King, Jr., and *Liberty and Sexuality: The Right to Privacy and the Making of Roe v. Wade.*

Notes

1. See generally Flora Davis, *Moving the Mountain: The Women's Movement in America Since 1960* (New York: Simon & Schuster, 1991). The movement's landmark book appeared only in 1963. See Betty Friedan, *The Feminine Mystique* (New York: W. W. Norton & Co., 1963); also see Daniel Horowitz, *Betty Friedan and the Making of The Feminine Mystique* (Amherst: University of Massachusetts Press, 1998), and Judith Adler Hennessee, *Betty Friedan: Her Life* (New York: Random House, 1999).

2. See for example John Egerton, *Speak Now Against the Day: The Generation Before the Civil Rights Movement in the South* (New York: Alfred A. Knopf, 1994), and my somewhat critical review of it, "A Day Late?" *Southern Changes* 17 (Spring 1995): 20–22. Also note Morton Sosna, *In Search of the Silent South: Southern Liberals and the Race Issue* (New York: Columbia University Press, 1977).

3. See Hollinger F. Barnard, ed., *Outside the Magic Circle: The Autobiography of Virginia Foster Durr* (Tuscaloosa: University of Alabama Press, 1985), and John A. Salmond, *The Conscience of a Lawyer: Clifford J. Durr and American Civil Liberties, 1899–1975* (Tuscaloosa: University of Alabama Press, 1990). Also note Sarah Hart Brown, *Standing Against Dragons: Three Southern Lawyers in an Era of Fear* (Baton Rouge: Louisiana State University Press, 1998).

4. See Tinsley E. Yarbrough, *A Passion for Justice: J. Waties Waring and Civil Rights* (New York: Oxford University Press, 1987).

5. See Myles Horton, *The Long Haul: An Autobiography* (New York: Doubleday, 1990), Aimee Isgrig Horton, *The Highlander Folk School* (Brooklyn, NY: Carlson Publishing, 1989), John M. Glen, *Highlander: No Ordinary School, 1932–1962* (Lexington: University Press of Kentucky, 1988), and Frank Adams, *Unearthing Seeds of Fire: The Idea of Highlander* (Winston-Salem, NC: John F. Blair, 1975).

6. See Frank Adams, *James A. Dombrowski: An American Heretic, 1897–1983* (Knoxville: University of Tennessee Press, 1992), Irwin Klibaner, *Conscience of a Troubled South: The Southern Conference Educational Fund, 1946–1966*

(Brooklyn, NY: Carlson Publishing, 1989), and Anthony P. Dunbar, *Against the Grain: Southern Radicals and Prophets, 1929–1959* (Charlottesville: University Press of Virginia, 1981).

7. See Anne C. Loveland, *Lillian Smith: A Southerner Confronting the South* (Baton Rouge: Louisiana State University Press, 1986), and Margaret Rose Gladney, ed., *How Am I to Be Heard? Letters of Lillian Smith* (Chapel Hill: University of North Carolina Press, 1993).

8. Unfortunately the only biography is Harold Martin, *William Berry Hartsfield: Mayor of Atlanta* (Athens: University of Georgia Press, 1978).

9. See Herbert T. Jenkins, *Keeping the Peace: A Police Chief Looks at His Job* (New York: Harper & Row, 1970), Herbert T. Jenkins, *Forty Years on the Force: 1932–1972* (Atlanta: Center for Research in Social Change, Emory University, 1973), and Herbert T. Jenkins, *Presidents, Politics and Policing* (Atlanta: Center for Research in Social Change, Emory University, 1980).

10. Maddox, of course, was subsequently elected governor of Georgia in 1966. See Lester Maddox, *Speaking Out: The Autobiography of Lester Garfield Maddox* (Garden City, NY: Doubleday, 1975), and Bruce Galphin, *The Riddle of Lester Maddox* (Atlanta: Camelot Publishing, 1968).

11. See Gary M. Pomerantz, *Where Peachtree Meets Sweet Auburn* (New York: Scribner, 1996), pp. 217, 287–300. See also Ivan Allen, Jr., with Paul Hemphill, *Mayor: Notes on the Sixties* (New York: Simon & Schuster, 1971).

12. See especially David J. Garrow, ed., *The Montgomery Bus Boycott and the Women Who Started It: The Memoir of JoAnn Gibson Robinson* (Knoxville: University of Tennessee Press, 1987), Charles Payne, *I've Got the Light of Freedom: The Organizing Tradition and the Mississippi Freedom Struggle* (Berkeley: University of California Press, 1995), Belinda Robnett, *How Long? How Long? African-American Women in the Struggle for Civil Rights* (New York: Oxford University Press, 1997), and Vicki L. Crawford et al., *Women in the Civil Rights Movement: Trailblazers and Torchbearers, 1941–1965* (Brooklyn: Carlson Publishing, 1990). Also note Lorraine Nelson Spritzer and Jean B. Bergmark, *Grace Towns Hamilton and the Politics of Southern Change* (Athens: University of Georgia Press, 1997), Cynthia Griggs Fleming, *Soon We Will Not Cry: The Liberation of Ruby Doris Smith Robinson* (Lanham, MD: Rowman & Littlefield, 1998), Linda O. McMurry, *To Keep the Waters Troubled: The Life of Ida B. Wells* (New York: Oxford University Press, 1998), and Chana Kai Lee, *For*

Freedom's Sake: The Life of Fannie Lou Hamer (Urbana: University of Illinois Press, 1999).

13. See Eliza K. Paschall, *It Must Have Rained* (Atlanta: Center for Research in Social Change, Emory University, 1975), Kathryn L. Nasstrom, *Everybody's Grandmother and Nobody's Fool: Frances Freeborn Pauley and the Struggle for Social Justice* (Ithaca: Cornell University Press, 2000), and, on Helen Bullard, Pomerantz, *Where Peachtree Meets Sweet Auburn.* Also note Kathryn L. Nasstrom, "Beginnings and Endings: Life Stories and the Periodization of the Civil Rights Movement," *Journal of American History* 86 (September 1999): 700–711.

14. Autobiographically, in addition to Ivan Allen's *Mayor* and Herbert Jenkins's books cited in note 9 above, see Morris B. Abram, *The Day Is Short* (New York: Harcourt Brace Jovanovich, 1982).

Some of the earliest studies of modern Atlanta political life are nowadays too infrequently cited. See Floyd Hunter, *Community Power Structure: A Study of Decision Makers* (Chapel Hill: University of North Carolina Press, 1953), M. Kent Jennings, *Community Influentials: The Elites of Atlanta* (New York: Free Press, 1964), and especially Floyd Hunter, *Community Power Succession: Atlanta's Policy-Makers Revisited* (Chapel Hill: University of North Carolina Press, 1980).

The four most important subsequent books on the city are Clarence N. Stone, *Regime Politics: Governing Atlanta, 1946–1988* (Lawrence: University Press of Kansas, 1989), Ronald H. Bayor, *Race and the Shaping of Twentieth Century Atlanta* (Chapel Hill: University of North Carolina Press, 1996), Gary Pomerantz's *Where Peachtree Meets Sweet Auburn,* cited above, and Charles Rutheiser's wonderfully insightful and provocative *Imagineering Atlanta: The Politics of Place in the City of Dreams* (New York: Verso, 1996). Also note Clarence N. Stone, *Economic Growth and Neighborhood Discontent: System Bias in the Urban Renewal Program of Atlanta* (Chapel Hill: University of North Carolina Press, 1976), Clifford M. Kuhn et al., *Living Atlanta: An Oral History of the City, 1914–1948* (Athens: University of Georgia Press, 1990), and Frederick Allen, *Atlanta Rising: The Invention of an International City, 1940–1990* (Atlanta: Longstreet Press, 1996).

The best starting points for Atlanta's specifically "civil rights" history in the 1960s are the essays by Jack L. Walker, Vincent D. Fort, and others reprinted in David J. Garrow, ed., *Atlanta, Georgia, 1960–1961: Sit-Ins and Stu-*

dent Activism (Brooklyn: Carlson Publishing, 1989), David A. Harmon, *Beneath the Image of the Civil Rights Movement and Race Relations: Atlanta, Georgia, 1946–1981* (New York: Garland, 1996), which includes a superb bibliography of little-known articles and theses dealing with Atlanta, and Kathryn L. Nasstrom, "Down to Now: Memory, Narrative, and Women's Leadership in the Civil Rights Movement in Atlanta, Georgia," *Gender & History* 11 (April 1999): 113–144. Also note Kathryn L. Nasstrom, "Women, the Civil Rights Movement, and the Politics of Historical Memory in Atlanta, 1946–1973" (Unpublished Ph.D. dissertation, University of North Carolina at Chapel Hill, 1993), and Melissa Fay Greene, *The Temple Bombing* (Reading, MA: Addison-Wesley, 1996). For subsequent developments, see Tamar Jacoby, *Someone Else's House* (New York: Free Press, 1998), pp. 357–529. Two biographies of important Atlantans are Janice Rothschild Blumberg, *One Voice: Rabbi Jacob M. Rothschild and the Troubled South* (Macon, GA: Mercer University Press, 1985), and Barbara B. Clowse, *Ralph McGill: A Biography* (Macon, GA: Mercer University Press, 1998).

15. See especially Sara M. Evans, *Personal Politics* (New York: Alfred A. Knopf, 1979).

16. Eddie Barker, "Advice to New Politician May Pay Off in September," *Atlanta Constitution,* 22 August 1961, p. 5.

17. Jean Rooney, "A Lot of Soul-Searching Went Into Her Decision," *Atlanta Constitution,* 23 August 1961, p. 17 ("I did plenty of soul-searching before I made up my mind").

18. Charles Moore, "3 Out of 4 Returned to School Unit," *Atlanta Constitution,* 14 September 1961, pp. 1, 8. Also see Doris Lockerman, "Women Politicos Fought With Dignity and Purpose," *Atlanta Constitution,* 13 September 1961, p. 20, and Doris Lockerman, "She's Been Running Scared and Polite." *Atlanta Constitution,* 21 September 1961, p. 20.

19. "An Editorial," *Atlanta Constitution,* 22 September 1961, p. 1.

20. Jack Strong, "Mitchell Gets School Board Seat," *Atlanta Constitution,* 23 September 1961, pp. 1, 8, "Mrs. Mitchell Gets School Post," *Atlanta Journal,* 23 September 1961, p. 3.

21. See "Public Held At Fault for Poor Schools," *Atlanta Constitution,* 13 December 1961, p. 9. Also see Margaret Turner, "Female 'Bill Watchers' Keep Eye on Law Making," *Atlanta Journal,* 28 December 1961, p. 33.

22. See Pat Watters, "A Visit to the Fourth Grade Tells A Bit of What Their

Life Is Like," *Atlanta Journal,* 11 December 1962, p. 28. Also note Sara Perry Mitchell, "Answers Given to Critics of U.N. Week Recently Observed in the City Schools," *Atlanta Constitution,* 6 December 1962, p. 4.

23. See Sara Mitchell, as told to Andrew Sparks, "Is High School Football Worth the Cost?" *Atlanta Journal Constitution Magazine,* 24 March 1963, pp. 10–11, 16.

24. See Pat Watters, "These Are Simplest, Most Basic Requirements for a Good School," *Atlanta Journal,* 26 March 1963, p. 18. Also note Doris Lockerman, "Is Education Trying to Do Too Much with Too Little?" *Atlanta Constitution,* 7 February 1963, p. 22.

25. John Heritage, "Mrs. Mitchell Rips Negro School Setup," *Atlanta Constitution,* 9 July 1963, pp. 1, 7. Also see Paul Valentine, "School Panel Official Hits Cost of Keeping Segregation," *Atlanta Journal,* 9 July 1963, p. 2. For accounts of Atlanta's excruciatingly slow progress with school desegregation during the 1960s, see Henry Mark Huie, "Factors Influencing the Desegregation Process in the Atlanta School System, 1954–1967" (Unpublished Ed.D. dissertation, University of Georgia, 1967), Susan M. McGrath, "Great Expectations: The History of School Desegregation in Atlanta and Boston, 1954–1990" (Unpublished Ph.D. dissertation, Emory University, 1992), and Paul E. Mertz, " 'Mind Changing Time All Over Georgia': HOPE, Inc., and School Desegregation, 1958–1961," *Georgia Historical Quarterly* 77 (Spring 1993): 41–61.

26. See "Racial Solutions Held Church Job," *Atlanta Journal,* 16 July 1963, pp. 1, 4, and "Mrs. Mitchell Raps Church Racial Bias," *Atlanta Constitution,* 17 July 1963, p. 6. Also note Doris Lockerman, "Woman Educator Soon Will Learn Price of Integrity," *Atlanta Constitution,* 18 July 1963, p. 23.

27. Frank Daniel, "Convictions Involve Her in Controversy," *Atlanta Journal Constitution,* 11 August 1963, p. C1.

28. See Walter Rugaber, "Increase Seen In Integration of Schools," *Atlanta Journal,* 7 April 1964, p. 2, Sara Mitchell, "School Board Member Against Ward System," *Atlanta Journal,* 22 December 1964, p. 22, and Doris Lockerman, "Mrs. Mitchell Says School Board Isn't Doing Its Key Job," *Atlanta Constitution,* 28 July 1964, p. 13.

29. See Marion Gaines, "12 Good Neighbors of Year Honored by Christians, Jews," *Atlanta Constitution,* 23 February 1965, p. 16.

30. See Celestine Sibley, "First Battle in War on Poverty Is Learning Names of Weapons," *Atlanta Constitution,* 14 May 1965, p. 5.

31. See Paul Ryan, "Mrs. Mitchell Says School Data Withheld," *Atlanta Constitution,* 18 October 1968, p. 8.

32. See "City School Board Loses Its 'Loner,'" *Atlanta Constitution,* 31 December 1968, p. 39. The story characterized Mitchell as "often a loner on the nine-member board."

33. See Sara Mitchell Parsons, "Shortage at Home," *Atlanta Journal,* 4 March 1998, p. A17, and Sara Mitchell Parsons, "King Family is Simply Seeking Justice," *Atlanta Journal Constitution,* 20 September 1998, p. R8.

34. Sara Mitchell Parsons, "School Vouchers No Solution," *Atlanta Journal,* 27 May 1999, p. A27.

Introduction

I first met Martin Luther King, Jr., on a spring day in April 1963. When I arrived at his church office on Auburn Avenue, the street was quiet. Only a few cars were in sight. I parked in front and entered through the big, heavy wooden double doors, which stood open. I walked up the few steps in the vestibule to Dr. King's large but sparsely furnished office. His door was also open. I walked in unannounced.

When I entered the office, I saw bare wooden floors, a much used desk, and a worn swivel chair that creaked when Dr. King moved. On the wall hung a large calendar with notes about upcoming church events. Books and papers lay scattered across the desk, on a long library table, and on top of the old-fashioned steam radiator. Dr. King got up from his desk, walked toward me smiling, and held out his hand.

He was a short, quiet man with piercing dark eyes. I had seen his face many times in news photos and on television, but somehow I was unprepared to find him in person intense and strong willed yet at the same time friendly, pleasant, and gentle. We shook hands, and I smiled back at him. For a moment I was unnerved.

The *Constitution* had reported Dr. King's arrival in Atlanta three years earlier, on January 24, 1960. The announcement noted merely that Dr. King was coming to assume the copastorate of Ebenezer Baptist Church with his father. Knowledgeable readers were well aware of other reasons for the move, however. Dr. King's former home in

Montgomery, Alabama, was an out-of-the-way location for the fledgling civil rights movement. Atlanta had a large, supportive, long-established power base of black educators, business leaders, and clergy. In Atlanta's black community, too, the King family was well known and highly respected.

Although the *Atlanta Constitution* was considered liberal, Dr. King's arrival in 1960 rated only six lines on a back page. The paper may have been reluctant to draw attention to the civil rights movement. In 1962 Dr. King would be arrested, tried, and convicted for leading a prayer vigil in front of the city hall in Albany, Georgia. In the early 1960s, sit-ins and protest demonstrations were taking place all over the South. Atlanta's white population was perhaps understandably quick to detect threats to the so-called southern way of life.

In 1960, however, I found the published account of Dr. King's arrival in Atlanta insufficient, given Dr. King's great importance. How had I, a native white southerner raised in a sea of southern bigotry, reached this point in my thinking?

Many years later, in 1990, I watched the moving and beautifully filmed television documentary *The Civil War* by Ken Burns. Night after night, I noticed that the dates of the battles—1861 to 1865—paralleled landmark events 100 years later in the civil rights movement. The two periods of turmoil seemed to have much in common.

In both the Civil War and the civil rights movement, the seeds of discontent and rebellion had been planted long before overt conflict and had persisted for many years afterward. At the end of the twentieth century, many northerners believe that the South has never stopped fighting the Civil War. By the same token, signs of racism and discrimination remain to the present day.

The Civil War produced awful devastation. Sixteen percent of all southern males lost their lives during just four years. Loving families have preserved the diaries and letters of ordinary soldiers and officers, mothers, brothers and sisters, sweethearts, and wives for over 100 years. These documents with their haunting words remind me of my own diaries, newspaper clippings, and correspondence from people prominent during the civil rights era, from Martin Luther King, Jr., and his wife, Coretta King, to the arch-segregationist Lester Maddox and members of the Ku Klux Klan. I regard the civil rights movement as the "Second Battle of Atlanta."

Although my ancestors were born and raised in the Deep South for generations, I never agreed with the aims of the Civil War. In my opinion, my distant kin were wrong. Despite their loyalty to the South and their bravery, they were driven at best by misplaced bravado and egotism and at worst by a desire to keep slavery alive. None of my ancestors was rich enough to own any slaves, thank goodness.

As a white southern woman, I came to the civil rights movement through a long process of self-discovery. I heard Dr. King and his father preach on many Sunday mornings. My most deeply held beliefs of fairness and equality led me to activism and then to elected office from 1962 until 1969. I was a guest in the Kings' home. To this day I remain friends with Coretta Scott King and other civil rights veterans.

In this book I tell of my encounters with segregationists and liberals, with Bible-toting Christians, with bigoted politicians and school administrators, and with Atlantans black and white who suddenly found themselves thrown together, torn between hate and love just like the soldiers in the Civil War that pitted brother against brother. I want readers to see the movement and its key personalities from my perspective as a woman and a southerner. This is the civil rights era as I remember it.

From Southern Wrongs to Civil Rights

I

Growing Up Southern

I was born Sara Bedell Perry in my grandmother's house on April 18, 1912, just three days after the *Titanic* went down. It was quite common at the time for a woman to "go home" to have her children, so my mother traveled a little farther east to Canton, Georgia, where my grandmother lived, and returned to my father after my birth. My mother and father already had two children and an established household in Cartersville, Georgia, a small town about thirty miles northwest of Atlanta.

My family on both sides had been southern born and bred for generations. My grandmother used to tell me about the Civil War. She said that we had had to leave the family farm when Yankee soldiers commandeered our house and land to stay in. After the army had moved on, we returned to find that the Yankees had put feed for their horses in our bureau drawers. Since there was no food to eat, her mother had knocked loose the grain from the bureau drawers onto a sheet and made cornbread for our homecoming meal. As a child I grew up playing with worthless Confederate money my grandmother's family had saved in a cigar box. I was raised as a daughter of the Old South.

In the early 1900s, my father's father owned a couple of small-town newspapers, and my father helped out. He became a kind of troubleshooting newspaper businessman, doing whatever it took to fix up ailing papers. He also dabbled in real estate. I remember that we moved from town to town a lot when I was little.

My mother was the typical dutiful wife of the era. My mother hated dirt. Everything had to be spotlessly clean—our house, our yard, even our sidewalk. Our bodies and clothes were always scrubbed and fresh. I got my first spanking at the age of three after I slid down a muddy bank wearing my Sunday school clothes.

My mother ran the household, raised the kids, and went to church. She was a strict Methodist. Her unthinking prejudice extended not only to blacks but also to Jews, Catholics, and Gypsies. Her fear of Gypsies was palpable. "They kidnap children," she warned us. "If you ever even *hear* a Gypsy caravan, you come in this house *immediately.*"

Lo and behold, when I was six my brother and sister actually did hear the dreaded sound. The caravan seemed headed right for our house! We ran inside as fast as we could and hid under our parents' bed. When curiosity finally got the best of us, we cautiously peeked through the curtains in the front bedroom. In the yard we saw wagons with pots and pans swinging from the sides, strange, exotic clothes in shades of the brightest yellows, oranges, and reds, and colorful beads and bracelets. Heads were swathed in bandannas. The Gypsies wore sandals on their bare, dusty feet.

In my southern community we feared others who were in any way different from us. I didn't even know a Catholic or Jew until we moved to Atlanta in 1925. And although blacks lived among us, they were fundamentally, profoundly different, or so I was constantly told. To most southern whites the black race seemed to have been brought to America to be our servants and farmhands. Most white families in the area had a black servant. Although my family was by no means rich, we were no exception. Our servant's name was Bertha, and she was the first black I ever knew. Right up to the 1950s, there was a kind, quiet, humble black woman in the life of most white children in the South.

Bertha was at our house every morning at about 6:30. She cooked breakfast and prepared a big dinner for the middle of the day. My mother sometimes allowed Bertha to go home for a few hours before she had to serve a light supper at six. Bertha could walk home. Each neighborhood had a section of small cabins nearby where servants lived. There was no public transportation, and no servant had a car.

My first distinct memory of Bertha dates to a warm spring afternoon in 1918, when I was six and my mother let me go home with Bertha. She lived in one of eleven identical cabins built in a row. Each was whitewashed, which was as near as servants' houses came to being painted. I did not see a black person living in a painted house until I moved to Atlanta in 1925.

I recall holding Bertha's hand as we walked down the sandy, dusty lane toward her cabin. Its one room was dark and smelled of wood smoke. There was a fireplace made of rough-laid bricks. To keep the cold winter winds from blowing through her cabin's wood plank walls, Bertha had pasted lots of brightly colored Sunday comics over the cracks. I found these comics fascinating.

I saw cast-off chairs, an old table, and a lumpy featherbed—or was the mattress made of corn shucks? A cardboard fan advertising an undertaker's parlor hung on a wall. Since there were no screens in the windows, Bertha used the fan as much to shoo away flies as to stir up any faint breeze.

What impressed me most was the big, humpbacked trunk that sat at the foot of Bertha's bed. It looked very mysterious, and I imagined all kinds of wonderful contents. Could it contain a beautiful wedding dress that had belonged to Bertha's mother? A long white baby dress and cap, handmade with lace and ribbons? But even as a six-year-old, I knew deep down inside that black servants were "dirt poor"—too poor to own any such treasures.

Bertha and I sat down at the table. She heaved a sigh of relief to be off her aching feet. It was no wonder they hurt. Servants in those days wore old, worn-out shoes and hand-me-down clothes acquired from some white family. In those days I don't recall ever seeing a black woman with a coat that was new or even quite her size. I don't recall what Bertha and I talked about, but I do remember feeling sorry for her.

Bertha was our daily cook, so she didn't do our washing. That back-breaking, time-consuming work fell to another black woman whose name I can't remember. Our washwoman came once a week and picked up our dirty clothes. She cleaned the clothes by boiling them in a big black iron pot in her yard and then hanging them out to dry. Next they were starched and painstakingly ironed with rock-heavy irons that were heated on top of a hot woodstove even on the hottest summer day.

I vividly remember how thin and tired our washwoman always looked. When she came to deliver our starched, pressed clothes each week, she was accompanied by her small son, who walked slowly behind her, pulling the large, heavy basket in a rickety wooden wagon. For all her labor, the washwoman was paid $1.50, a woefully inadequate sum. One time, I saw my mother take some hard candy from her pocket and hand it to the washwoman and her son. Was this from kindness, I wondered, or was it because my mother felt guilty for paying her so little?

Most southerners will say that they seldom heard or even used the word "prejudice." We lived without thinking, for the most part blindly ignorant of our multiple sins against blacks. At the same time prejudice was as strong and widespread in our lives as terminal cancer. It would take a vast library to hold all the examples of white people's prejudice against blacks before the civil rights movement and afterward.

When I was about nine I recall seeing a black girl riding a girl's bicycle. The sight was memorable because no black family in Greenwood, South Carolina, in the early 1920s could have afforded such a luxury.

It would be hard for any white person to write a definitive history of black woman servants before the 1960s—cooks, maids, and so-called nannies. The truth about this complex subject lurks in dark corners almost impossible to explore. Fanny Kemble, the English wife of a southern plantation owner, came close, but her book, *Journal of a Resident on a Georgia Plantation,* was published in 1863. She told the true story of slave women, how they were bought and sold with no thought given to their personal lives and how they were cruelly separated from their husbands and children when family members were sold to plantation owners living miles away.

I learned the most about servants and the way they were treated in my own home and in those of friends. Until World War II nearly every middle-class southern family could afford to hire a servant or at least part-time help. A family that was well off could afford to hire several servants. In the 1930s and 1940s servants came to back doors, hat in hand, smiling, to ask even the smallest favor—a degrading custom indeed.

Although their weekly salaries amounted to near starvation wages, servants were almost never given a raise, no matter how faithful they had been or how hard they had tried to please. What did they think when they couldn't afford to pay anyone to stay with their children while they took care of ours? How did they feel about our elaborate dinner and cocktail parties, tables laden with food, when their own family often went hungry?

I don't know the answers to these questions. I never asked. I can only wonder why our servants did not hate us. No doubt many of them did. All these years later I can only marvel at the love and patience they showed me—love in spite of our unseeing, unthinking, indifferent treatment. Even if we were kind, and even if we did "love" them, what kind of love did we offer them?

Once Martin Luther King listened while a white woman raved on and on to him about how much she loved Inez, her servant. "What is Inez's last name?" he asked. The woman did not know even though Inez had been with her family for twenty years.

My grandmother had a cook named Mary who was kind, cheerful, overworked, and grossly underpaid. How she kept body and soul together on her salary of five dollars a week remains a mystery to me. One Christmas Mary somehow managed to give everyone in our family a gift. The small blue glass vase she gave me touched my heart more than any other present I received that year.

During the 1920s and 1930s servants were paid so little that by unspoken agreement they were allowed to tote home any leftover food from the evening meal. This privilege was no doubt granted to help ease the guilt we felt for their low wages—or perhaps we knew in our hearts that without this food their families would go hungry. Mary toted leftovers in a large round tin pan covered with newspapers and tied tightly with heavy string to keep the food warm. On rainy days she would carefully wrap the tin in an extra cover of wax paper. Mary had to walk to the streetcar, then ride across town to the black section eight miles away. More often than not she probably stood in the back after having been on her feet for the better part of ten hours.

I wish I had been older when Mary worked for my grandmother. At the time I was a teenager more interested in boys than in what went on inside our house. But I did realize that Mary was different from any blacks I had known before. She was better spoken and had a better grasp of what was going on in the world. It was fun and interesting for me to talk with her.

In the 1940s, years after Mary had left us to go to work for one of our cousins in Washington, D.C. (where the pay was much better), she came back to visit relatives in Atlanta and stopped by to see my mother and me. She had moved to New York and married a well-off Chinese merchant. When she entered our house, she was wearing a full-length fur coat. Despite the change in her fortunes, she was still the same caring Mary we remembered, and there was much affection all around as we visited.

According to a southern tradition, whenever a family servant left a position, she always recommended someone—usually a relative—to take her place. There were no employment agencies, because this networking was satisfactory to both parties. When Mary left us to go to

Washington, she sent us her cousin Ruby. Ruby was very lively and had a boyfriend named Oscar, who, as we said in the 1930s, "could play a mean piano." One party my sister and I threw must have been quite special, because not only did Ruby come back to serve a late meal, she brought Oscar to play our old upright piano in the parlor. I wonder what we paid Oscar for his three hours of playing.

Ruby, like Mary, hoped for a better life, so she too left Atlanta for a job up north (as did hundreds of thousands of other blacks). My mother wrote her a nice letter of recommendation, and Ruby sent her a thank-you note. It was the only letter my mother ever got from a black person, and she kept it until she died forty years later. The letter, mailed from Philadelphia on October 22, 1943, still has three one-cent stamps on it. It reads:

Dear Mrs. Perry,
You don't know how much I thank you for what you did for me. I couldn't have gotten my job without your help, Mrs. Perry—I really don't know how to thank you. I have met a lot of people since I have been up here but none of them compare to you. Because you always would help when it was needed and thanks a lot for making me save what I can.

Now I am working on a very good job. I am beginning this week to send money home to mother just as you know she needs it, Mrs. Perry. Again I want to thank you for what you did for me. I won't forget. Tell the family hello for me.

Respectfully,
Ruby

My family kept moving around, but I'd have to say I had a typical, happy southern childhood. I enjoyed school and was an average student. I had friends, played outside (but never with any black children), went to church, and saw relatives.

My parents had a troubled relationship, however. My father always seemed to be gone on business, sometimes for weeks at a time. He drank, he smoked big cigars, he played poker, and he ran with a racy crowd. My very straightlaced mother abhorred his activities. Mother's main goal was to raise her five children right in the sight of God and the community. I was the middle child. There was never any cursing or drinking or card playing in my mother's house. My father had to go elsewhere to pursue any of his favorite activities. Although she was stern, my mother was a kind, loving, generous person. She sang and read to us. She cared about our cultural and social lives.

Even as a ten-year-old, I could tell that my parents were not suited to each other. I remember asking my grandmother on my mother's side why my parents ever got married. She said, "I guess it was because your mother was the prettiest girl in her high school graduating class, and your father was the best looking. You know, in those days, boys and girls seldom indulged in any revealing conversations about themselves, so how could they have really known each other?" As I look back now on the huge differences between my parents—my mother's down-to-earth, religious lifestyle and my father's love of worldly pleasures—I can see why I grew up feeling so many contradictory impulses.

When I was thirteen, my parents divorced, and small-town life came to an abrupt end. In the mid-1920s, particularly among families that claimed to be respectable and church-going, divorce was an earth-shattering experience. My mother felt impelled to take the unthinkable initiative when my father sold our house to settle a business debt. The marriage ended when there was little money left and no house to live in. My mother, my two brothers, and my two sisters sought shelter with my grandmother, who had moved from her place in Canton to a large house in a pleasant middle-class neighborhood in Atlanta. We knew that there would be no going back to our small-town life or to our father. I remember thinking as we drove into town down Ponce de Leon Avenue, "I wonder what kind of life is ahead of me?"

I spent my teenage years in Atlanta. I went to the city's only public high school for girls, named Atlanta Girl's High. It was a school for whites. At the time I had no idea where—or even whether—black girls and boys went to high school in Atlanta. I had plenty of friends, both girls and boys. In those days everyone, especially young people, felt very optimistic and sophisticated. Yet our relationships were slow-paced, innocent and unthreatening. Dates usually involved going to dances or the movies or drive-ins for hot dogs.

The Great Depression hit Atlanta forcefully just a few months after my graduation in the spring of 1930. I was then eighteen. A couple of years earlier, my mother had taken a job as a sales clerk at Rich's, Atlanta's largest department store. Luckily, she was not laid off. It was the only job she ever had, and she kept it for thirty-eight years.

During the depression, our family finances were generally meager. We never received a dime of support from our father. College was out of the question for me. We were still living with my grandmother, and right out of high school I took a job with Retail Credit Company (now Equifax, a worldwide information services company). Even then Retail Credit generated tons of paperwork, so it needed lots of "girls" like me to type and file.

I sat in a huge room with probably twenty-five other girls, each of us at a desk with a big black manual typewriter. We typed or filed from 8:30 A.M. until 5:00 P.M. five days a week plus a half day on Saturday. It took me about thirty minutes to get to and from work on the street-car. I had many friends. We dated, went out for Cokes, and even made the trip to Candler Airfield (now Hartsfield International Airport), an exotic new place, to watch airplanes take off and land.

In 1932 my boss at Retail Credit Company—the head of the home office's personnel department—asked me out. Ray Mitchell was twenty-nine years old to my nineteen and was as handsome as a movie star. He had been in Emory University's first graduating class and was already a member of Atlanta's second most exclusive club, the Capital City Club. Ray dated debutantes, loved to dance, and clearly had a great professional career ahead of him. I was impressed! My mother was also impressed, not only with Ray's current success and prospects, but because he "came from good people," as we used to say. In fact, his family was every bit as purebred southern as ours. Like my great-grandfather, Ray's grandfather Mitchell had been in the Civil War.

The Mitchell family lived just a little north of Atlanta in a small farming community called Sandy Springs (today it's one of Atlanta's most prosperous suburbs). According to family lore, when Lee surrendered to Grant at Appomattox, Virginia, grandfather Mitchell walked home with a minnie ball still in his leg.

Mitchell and Hildebrand Roads in Sandy Springs are named after the two sides of Ray's family. Ray was born on Roswell Road, which is now a major commercial thoroughfare. Ray's father worked for Coca-Cola as a low-level manager. Ray was the oldest of eight children. His mother was a housewife and a strict Baptist who, like my own mother, refused to have liquor, cards, or smoking in her house. I can still see Ray's father sitting in the living room with an unlit cigar in his mouth. He went out on the porch to smoke.

Ray was high on the list of everybody in my family, including me. While we dated, I continued to work at my job. He remained the head of the personnel department. He never showed me any favoritism, and I never expected any. I don't remember hearing even a word of criticism from the other girls. Certainly no one thought of sexual harassment. It wasn't even a workplace concept in 1931.

Ray and I married on June 16, 1933. At the time of our wedding, Ray thought he was getting a sweet, polite, well-brought-up southern girl, someone who could be the mother of his children and a helpful adjunct to his professional career—someone who could move up with him in Atlanta society. In June of 1933, when I was twenty-one, he believed I was just such a person.

Not until the early 1950s did I become aware that a racial crisis was approaching and was becoming more severe with each passing day. I owe my awareness to Ralph McGill's column on page one of the

Atlanta Constitution. Again and again, McGill appealed to his readers to abandon their traditional segregated ways of living. When the crisis arrived at mid-decade, even the white Protestant and Catholic churches remained largely silent. McGill's was one of a very few voices of reason to be heard in the white community.

At the end of the 1950s, when I was becoming politically active in the civil rights movement, I felt sorry for Ray. The girl he had married no longer existed. I could understand Ray's frustration and anger. But I couldn't go back to being something that did not seem morally right to me.

While we were dating, I can't recall a single incident involving anything to do with race. Because Ray's family was so much from the country, Mrs. Mitchell did most of the cooking and cleaning and child rearing on her own. This work was, after all, her sole purpose in life. I don't ever remember seeing a maid or cook at Ray's house.

Race was a part of our everyday lives in Atlanta. Blacks were servants and laborers. Educated middle-class whites acted respectful toward them, never consciously put them down, and certainly never used the "n" word. I never once heard Ray use that low-class, belittling word, as conservative and even as prejudiced as I knew he was.

Practically from the day I married, black maids formed an integral part of our household. As a southern bride who had been raised in a household that always included a cook, I had never in my life prepared a real meal. In fact, I hardly even knew how to light the gas oven in our new duplex.

Then one day, out of the blue, one of my life's greatest blessings came with a simple knock on the door. There stood Letha Hood, a neat, attractive young black woman exactly my age. She said, "Excuse me, but I heard from the maid next door that you might be needing some help." Although my new husband handled all our financial matters, this question seemed to me part of household management, my responsibility. I felt desperate enough—and confident enough—to hire Letha on the spot. I didn't check references or even wonder whether she could cook (white people assumed that all black women could cook and "keep house"). I just liked her and hired her to come in for five half days a week (Thursdays and Sundays were her days off) from 12:00 noon until 6:30 P.M. Her salary was five dollars a week.

Watching Letha, I learned my way around staples of southern cooking such as fried chicken, rice and milk gravy, butter beans, and a host of other high-calorie, high-fat, high-cholesterol delicacies. Soon after Letha's arrival, I became pregnant with our first child. If Letha had been important in the household before, she became indispensable to me then and even more so after the birth of Ray, Jr.

When the baby was about a year old, we took Letha with us to New Orleans. We were going on a cruise and taking a vacation in Cuba. Ray's father had been transferred by Coca-Cola to New Orleans, so we were able to leave the baby with Ray's parents during our holiday. With Letha in a starched uniform holding the baby, we set off early one morning on the drive down. We stopped in some small town in Alabama for lunch. Letha, wearing her uniform, was obviously with us and was obviously holding our baby. I thought there would be no problem if she ate quietly with us. I was wrong.

I can still see the café owner walking over and hear his words. "We don't serve her kind. She's got to leave." We ordered for Letha and she ate her food in our hot car. I felt terribly sorry for her, though I made no scene. Why should she suffer such an indignity because of her skin color? In New Orleans, Letha stayed in the basement servant's quarters of Ray's parents' house. When we drove back to Atlanta, all three of us knew, without ever talking about it, that we must not take her into a restaurant again, uniform and baby or not.

Letha stayed with us for fifteen years, until 1948. I had three children, and I couldn't imagine coping without her loving, uncomplaining help. But one day, again out of the blue, Letha announced that she and her husband would be joining the northward migration. They were moving to Chicago. I tried to be understanding, but I was devastated. I remember going into our large pantry right after Letha left the kitchen and crying and crying. When I stopped long enough to look up, I saw a long row of canned red tomatoes. To this day, whenever I see such a can, I remember Letha's leaving.

The only other time I recall interacting with blacks early in my marriage involved Ray. In 1935 or 1936, the city sponsored a course meant to help blacks develop basic service skills. Because Ray was head of personnel for one of Atlanta's most prestigious companies, he was invited to attend the graduation. He asked me to accompany him. During the ceremony, one of the graduates came up to me and shook my hand. Although I was now twenty-four years old and had seen blacks every day all my life, I had never before shaken hands with a black.

Ray was gracious and courteous, but he believed that God had made white people superior to blacks. He would willingly go to any black function where the class lines were clearly drawn, where he, and any blacks who might be present, could be certain of his standing. He had no problem about attending our maid's wedding in the early 1950s, for instance, even though we were the only whites there.

My second child, a daughter named Susan Melinda, was born on April 19, 1936, one day after my twenty-fourth birthday. We had moved to a new house on Club Drive in the Buckhead section of Atlanta, just around the corner from the Capital City Country Club. Ray could walk to the golf course from our new home in a couple of minutes. At the time we were upwardly mobile. I was a happy, busy homemaker, involved in neighborhood activities, a garden club, two bridge clubs, Buckhead's most prominent Methodist church, and our two large families. Even the coming of World War II in December of 1941 had very little impact on our lives. Ray was almost thirty-nine and therefore too old for service. I had my third and final child, a boy named Perry. Perry was my maiden name. In the South it was common to use one's maiden name as a given name. Outwardly I was happy. But something deep down inside me was starting to stir, albeit very faintly.

2

From Buckhead to Brotherhood

I remember one night in 1943 going through my usual bedtime routine of reading and finding some popular music on the radio when by chance I heard an announcer intone, "This is the 'Town Hall of the Air,' a program of discussion and debate on the most important issues of the day."

I continued searching for music, but then I said to myself, "You're going to turn thirty years old next month—it's time for you to grow up. It's your turn to make a contribution to society, your turn to know and care about what is happening in the world outside yourself and your family." So I switched back to "Town Hall of the Air" and listened to the end. I no longer recall the issues discussed and debated, though in 1943 they probably related to World War II. But the program made a significant impression on me.

Not that my life changed forever, starting the very next morning. It didn't. Still, I had had a little epiphany that was the beginning of a long journey of consciousness raising, to borrow a term that wouldn't be in vogue for another twenty-five years. A year or two later, I reached another turning point after coming across an article in *Life* magazine about a champion bridge player. I began to wonder whether, with effort and study, I could become a world-class bridge player. I asked myself whether, if I could actually become a champion player, that was what I wanted. When I was gone, was that how I want my children to remember their mother? Or was there some better contribution I could make to the world, something more lasting I could do with my life? During this period, I was a devout Methodist and a Sunday school teacher. All my life I had been exhorted as a Christian to care about my fellow man. The message resonated more strongly now.

In April 1947 I suddenly felt compelled to attend an event that was in fact unprecedented in Atlanta. It was a political rally to hear former vice president Henry Wallace, one of the Democratic candidates for president. Wallace might have agreed to deliver another ho-hum stump speech. Instead, according to front-page headlines in both the *Atlanta Constitution* and the *Atlanta Journal,* Wallace had announced that he would speak only before an integrated audience. As far as I knew, the city had never since Reconstruction encountered such a situation. Any kind of public integration was unheard of in the South at that time.

The newspapers reported the city fathers' declaration that there was no hall, meeting room, or auditorium where a nonsegregated assembly could take place. In the ensuing dispute neither Wallace nor the city was prepared to relent. The stalemate lasted for three tension-filled days. Then the Reverend William Borders of the Wheat Street Baptist Church, one of Atlanta's best-known black ministers, invited Wallace to speak at his large sanctuary.

I got caught up in the excitement of this first-ever event and decided I had to attend. I now believe that this was a further stirring of my social conscience. I remember feeling both sad and mad that Atlanta's white leaders were putting blacks down in such a publicly humiliating way. What could possibly be wrong with letting people of both races sit in the same room at a political rally? But as soon as I had made up my mind that it was important for me to go, I realized that my husband would give me a hard time about it. Ray, like 90 percent of middle-class southern whites, was a Democrat through and through, but he never showed any interest in being politically active.

And to be honest, now that I think about it, this was the first political rally I had ever wanted to attend. Add the racial slant, and Ray's response when I broached the subject came as no surprise: "I will not go with you, and I will not hear of your going. No white woman should be allowed to go to 'colored' town alone, certainly not at night." He thought his word would be final, but I felt suddenly restless and determined to find a way. First I called Dr. Nat G. Long, our highly respected minister at Peachtree Road Methodist Church. I asked him if he would go with me. To his credit and in the spirit of Christianity, he agreed. Next, I called my mother, who was always accommodating where one of her children was concerned and who was doubly pleased whenever anything involved a minister. I asked her whether she would go with Dr. Long and me. She immediately agreed. As long as I traveled in such impeccable company, there wasn't much Ray could say. I had him outflanked. How could he refuse to let his wife go out with her mother and his minister?

The night arrived. The Wheat Street sanctuary was full. The audience was about two-thirds black and one-third white. I don't remember anything former vice president Wallace said, but I do remember sitting in the quiet, handsome church, thinking my own thoughts and crying silently. How could such a calm, innocent event have caused such an uproar and public outcry? Yet just by being there and showing my support for this unprecedented integrated gathering, I felt that a burden was being lifted, that something great, a long-awaited event, was starting to happen. At long last Atlantans of both races were meeting and sitting together in public, and the sky had not fallen!

I wish I could report that my life changed after I attended Atlanta's first public integrated meeting—that I came home, laid down the law to my conservative husband, and immediately devoted myself to the cause of racial equality. But I didn't. I had taken a few first steps, but I wasn't even sure where they were leading. Still, I did realize from time to time that I lived in a racially intolerant world, and how shocked I was when I saw evidence close to home. One day, when my older son, Ray, Jr., was about ten, he told me he had been playing at his best friend's house. He and his friend had discovered a Ku Klux Klan robe and peaked hood in the closet of his friend's father. I was appalled.

These were so-called nice people who lived just eight houses up the street from us on Club Drive. They went to our church!

Despite such jolts, I was fully settled in my comfortable suburban lifestyle. My two older children were in school, and my youngest was about to start. I went to my bridge clubs, the garden club, the neighborhood "study" club, and the country club. I taught Sunday school, ran the household (with our maid's full-time help), ferried kids to and fro, and did chores. I had plenty of energy and was always busy with projects, from sewing for my daughter and myself to painting rooms in the house.

My mother's favorite saying was "Idle hands are the devil's workshop." To be inactive was by definition to be lazy, or "no account," as we used to say. So I was very busy every day, but after my youngest child had been in school a couple of years—in about 1951, when I was thirty-nine—I realized once again that something wasn't right, that I needed to reexamine my life and how I was spending my time. One day I concluded that I was going in the wrong direction. I was so sure of the feeling that I sat right down at my desk and wrote letters of resignation to my two bridge clubs, the garden club, and the study club. I couldn't resign from the country club, because it was strictly my husband's bailiwick.

My friends couldn't understand why I would do anything so drastic. I still recall one telling comment: "Oh, Sara, you're just ruining your daughter's chance to make her debut!" I didn't tell Ray that I had dropped my clubs, but he sensed a change in me that made him uneasy—and with good reason, as things turned out. At first I wasn't even sure what I was going to do with my spare time, but on a very deep level, I knew I would get involved in something more meaningful than playing bridge with the girls or orchestrating my daughter's debut.

It never occurred to me to resign from my church. Such a step would have killed my mother, and in any case church was a fundamental part of my being. I enjoyed and was intellectually stimulated by the adult Sunday school class I had been teaching for over a decade. I also stayed active in my church's Women's Society. Ironically, this last group soon led me into politics.

After World War II, nearly every prayer at Peachtree Road Methodist ended in a fervent supplication to God to "bring everlasting peace to our nation." Although I heartily agreed with the sentiment, something about the prayers annoyed me. Even as I sat primly on the hard pew wearing my white gloves and hat, it seemed to me odd that although God did not get us into wars, we were asking Him to keep us out of one. After hearing one such prayer too many, I asked myself: Who declares war? Who is responsible? The answer seemed clear: the president, the senators, and the congressmen. And I knew full well who elected the politicians.

I began wondering how many members of our church were registered to vote. At the time, around 1953, I guessed that at most 70 percent of the men and about 30 percent of the women were registered. Women attended church more often than men, which meant that they were praying more, but they did not have the practical, here-on-earth impact that they might if they prayed a little less and voted more often.

Not long after these musings, I had a chance to influence women's voting habits. I was asked to chair a new committee of our church's Women's Society called the Status of Women Committee. The name was ironic, I thought, since women at the time had little status in the Methodist church. Women were responsible only for teaching children, keeping the nursery during church, and working at the Wednesday night church suppers. As chairperson, I found that I could persuade the committee members to register others in the Women's Society to vote.

The League of Women Voters seemed a logical place to start. I called its office and asked to have a member sent to our next meeting along with the county registrar. They came, set up a card table in the church vestibule, and registered some forty women that day. The success of the venture led me to my own personal early vision of a peaceful world that would last forever and would begin right here with the women of Peachtree Road Methodist Church.

From this point in 1953 onward, the steps in my long journey from complacent, middle-class southern housewife to liberal, integrationist politician came much more quickly. Once I started looking more closely at the world around me, I could never go back. In fact, what I saw made me realize that I could actually make a difference in the causes I believed in. A few people not only listened to my ideas but also complimented me on them—something my husband never did.

When I look back on this period of huge transition in my life, I realize that the sense of being heard, of being accepted as having a brain, and of being capable of leadership fueled my budding political activity. Ray wanted me to stay in all of the clubs, to be his housewife, his corporate wife, and his dancing partner at the country club—and nothing more. He hadn't married me for my brain and certainly not for any outspokenness.

I was getting a taste of intellectual praise, not only for my work on the Status of Women Committee and in my adult Sunday school class, but also in the PTA, where I had become active. Ray obviously didn't know it, but I had no intention of returning to the lifestyle he expected of me. In my opinion, I was becoming a much more interesting person, but I could understand his unease. Ray was clearly unwilling to let me grow and change.

In fact, my heart and mind were heading in a radically new direction. One day a church friend invited me to a monthly lunch meeting of the Atlanta League of Women Voters. Although I really wasn't much of a political activist, I reluctantly agreed to keep her company. I enjoyed the meeting, and when I learned that annual dues was one dollar, it seemed too good a bargain to pass up. Little did I know then how much that one dollar would change my life.

Membership in the League, I reasoned, wasn't just for my own pleasure. The new voters we had recruited needed to be informed on

the current political issues. As chairman of the Status of Women Committee, I felt I should join the League and receive its study guides,
which laid out both sides of important political issues coming up on
the local, state, and national scenes. With the League's help our group
could become informed voters.

The more I read about the League, the more I liked what it stood
for—the education of women on the most pressing issues of the day.
The League certainly opened my eyes, not only to the issues, but also
to the way the political process really worked from the ground up. I
learned how to make your support of an issue known to the right
people, what really went on when elected officials met, and what it
took to get legislation introduced and acted upon. I found all of this
activity exciting, challenging, and rewarding. I soon became active in
the League and was named chairman of the Education Committee. At
the time I had three children in public school and was president of
their high school PTA.

League meetings were held in a donated office in the Henry Grady,
a famous old downtown Atlanta hotel that stood where the circular
Westin Peachtree Plaza Hotel now stands. We used two windowless
rooms with faded pea green walls that looked as if they hadn't been
repainted since women got the right to vote. The desks and chairs
were practically Salvation Army rejects. The conference tables were
scarred and warped and fit awkwardly at best when they were pulled
together. We spent hours sitting on hard gray metal folding chairs, but
no one seemed to mind.

Every year, the various League chapters set an agenda for discussion
with special emphasis on local items. In 1954, our Atlanta chapter decided that we needed to study civil rights laws as they applied to public
education and that we needed to look at the issue from a racial viewpoint. The Supreme Court had only just ruled, in *Brown v. Board of
Education,* that "separate but equal" schools were not equal and vio-
lated the Constitution.

The Education Committee concluded that the League should support the concept of equal education for all children, regardless of race or economic status. Within weeks of our study, one single event occurred that more than anything else propelled me into the civil rights movement. We were having our 1956 annual meeting at the Atlanta Women's Club auditorium. I had just been nominated for my first term on the League's Board of Directors. From my spot in the audience I was extra-attentive to the proceedings. I was carefully watching and learning from the women on the platform because I expected to join them soon.

Out of one eye, I could see two newspaper reporters who looked bored. Our agenda included the nomination of officers for 1957, the treasurer's report, the next year's program study agenda, and proposed changes to the by-laws.

The meeting was proceeding smoothly when a new member, someone who had recently moved to Atlanta "from up north somewhere," rose from her seat and asked for "the privilege of the floor." In a strong, clear voice she said, "I see that this chapter's by-laws don't conform to the National League's." There was total silence. The newcomer had everyone's attention, but no one foresaw her next words: "Your by-laws state that any *white* woman may be a member. . . . I move that the word 'white' be stricken from the by-laws of the Atlanta League of Women Voters."

After the initial gasps, many of the 125 white members present wanted to speak. Long lines formed behind the two microphones in the aisles. Each woman had three minutes to state whether she was for or against the motion, give her reasons, and be seated. The League does not permit long-windedness.

One member—the good friend who had helped register voters at church and had persuaded me to attend my first League meeting—came to the mike and said, "The Atlanta League was the first chapter in the nation formed after women got the right to vote in 1920." Then her voice became emotional and high-pitched as she continued, "If we allow Negroes to join this proud organization, we will kill it."

The debate continued late into the afternoon. "The time has come for us to join the twentieth century," said some. Others declared, "I will never, *never* vote to accept Negro members." They pronounced "Negro" "nigra." I didn't go to the microphone. I listened. The more I heard, the more certain I became of where I stood.

Finally, a tired, impatient woman reached the mike and in a loud, authoritative voice said, "I move this body strike the word 'white' before the word 'member' in our by-laws." The motion was seconded and put to a vote. Joyfully and without hesitation, I shouted "Aye!" Although most of my friends in the League were on the opposite side, the organization-dividing motion passed and took effect immediately. The reporters, now fully alert, had a scoop. The segregation/integration problem was just starting to come to a head in Atlanta in 1956. Our meeting made front-page headlines in the evening papers and the morning ones. The wire services—AP and UPI—both picked it up. *Time* also reported on our actions.

The chapter's president, vice president, and six board members resigned right after the vote had been taken. Four board members remained. The women who resigned vowed to start a new, all-white organization, and they wasted no time whatsoever. Instead of going home like the rest of us after the long, exhausting meeting, they hurried back to our office, took the membership files, and even got a locksmith to change the door locks immediately. During the ensuing weeks they formed a new organization, the Atlanta Voters Guild, which was of course lily white. I think it lasted a few years before disappearing.

When we found ourselves locked out of the League office, one of the members on our side called a lawyer. We learned that as the sanctioned chapter we had legal rights to the office, so we called another locksmith and had him reopen the office the next morning. Then we met and made plans to regroup and elect new officers and board members. I was elected vice president. A friend later remarked, "You sure did rise fast in the League's hierarchy!" And indeed I had, though not because of my own initiative.

After all the publicity had subsided, we worried that our losses would be severe. The organization had had more than 1,000 members before the annual meeting. Immediately afterward several hundred members had resigned. How many more would join them? We also worried that we would be unable to find a place to hold large meetings, including our luncheon meetings, as an integrated organization in a segregated city. Would our main financial supporters, Atlanta's businessmen, continue their donations? Would the owners of the old-line Henry Grady Hotel kick us out of our rent-free office? And I had concerns even closer to home. How would my traditional, conservative husband react to my involvement in this highly publicized affair?

As it turned out, the majority of our members were wildly supportive. Starting the very next morning we found ourselves swamped with outside phone calls from new recruits. Typical comments were, "I've never joined the League, but now I can't wait," "I didn't know the League had such gutsy members," "Count me in for a lifetime membership," "I'm sending money right away," and "I'm available to help out at the office anytime."

The owners of the Henry Grady Hotel, much to their credit, allowed us to stay in our space, but we did have to relocate our monthly luncheon meetings, which had been held at Atlanta's most prestigious—and restricted—Piedmont Driving Club. Hearing of our plight, the Jewish Progressive Club quickly offered their handsome meeting facilities.

When the public learned that the Atlanta League was truly open to all women, regardless of their skin color, four black women joined immediately. Each of them might have been elected woman of the year. Grace Hamilton later became the first black woman to serve in the Georgia legislature. Myrtle Davis later became president of the Atlanta League and then an Atlanta City Council member for many years. Johnnie Yancey spearheaded Atlanta University's Student Voter Registration Project. Cassandra Maxwell Bernie was a lawyer.

These outstanding women spoke to the rest of us about the many, many problems facing their segregated neighborhoods: restrictive zoning, crowded housing, unpaved streets, lack of city water in some areas, and—most important to me—schools that were second-class in every way, from ancient textbooks to inadequate and unkempt grounds. League study groups had long felt overwhelmed by the many problems on the white side of town. Now we were suddenly learning of much worse problems in the black neighborhoods.

Our eyes were being opened, and we were making a beginning. Grace Hamilton agreed to serve on the Education Committee. She arrived at her first meeting with a large map showing the location of all the public schools in Atlanta. The more we looked at it, the more puzzled we became. Seeing our confusion, Grace laughed. "Here's your problem," she told us. "On your map, the white schools are marked with white circles, and the black schools with black circles, but on our map, we marked the white schools with black circles, and the black ones with white circles. We have our fun where we can!" Everyone laughed.

During these difficult times there were a few meeting places where the races could mingle and exchange ideas. One of these was the Hungry Club on Butler Street, around the corner from Auburn Avenue in the heart of the black business district. Although Atlanta was totally segregated, somehow it was permissible for whites to attend the Hungry Club as speakers. At lunchtime blacks and whites met there weekly, not for food but to share news of the city.

With these developments, my once proper, quiet social life became both controversial and public. Suddenly there was much to do, and I had time to spare. My oldest son had graduated from the University of Georgia and was already married. My daughter was attending the University of Alabama. My younger son though still at home was in high school, and Ray worked from 8:30 A.M. until 4:30 P.M. With

everyone out of the house most of each day I felt free to spend countless hours at the League office and at League meetings.

Back on the home front, however, my new activities created growing tension between Ray and me. Ray became quite worried about my
public image, which from his point of view was questionable and
reflected on him. I could understand Ray's concern. In those days,
married women were always known by their husband's name. It was
"Mrs. John Doe," not "Mrs. Mary Doe." I tried to reassure him by
explaining that I was merely representing the League's views. Didn't
he agree that it was a worthwhile and highly respected organization?
He reluctantly replied, "All right. Just don't get our name on the front
page again. I don't ever want my name associated with any racial controversy again." I promised to be careful. Still, I felt hurt and even a
little resentful. Ray had never given me one word of praise, not even
for standing up for something I believed in strongly.

As fate would have it, hardly a week passed before my face appeared
on the front page of the *Atlanta Journal*. I was standing in the rear of a
room in the state capitol where there was a hearing underway on Atlanta's land-use plan, then under study by the League. Blacks were
arguing that the plan restricted them to just 15 percent of the city's
land although they accounted for nearly 40 percent of the total population.

I was so absorbed in the proceedings that I didn't notice the prim,
neatly dressed white woman sitting near me until she jumped up and
in a loud, shrill voice began vilifying "niggers." The television news
crews and the still photographers immediately swung their cameras
around to focus on her and in the process caught me full in the face.
There I was in the background, a nameless but conspicuous member
of the audience. When Ray saw the shot on the front page that evening,
I said, "You only told me to keep our name off the front page, not my
picture!" He was not amused.

My League involvement was quickly changing both my personality
and my life. I forgot my former shyness. Now I wasn't afraid to debate

issues with city council members, county commissioners, state legislators, and even the governor of Georgia.

My first encounter with the governor was passive and solitary, although very emotional for me. Ernest Vandiver was sworn in at the state capitol on January 14, 1957, a year after the state legislature had voted to change Georgia's flag so that it featured the blatantly racist Confederate "stars and bars" design. He was a segregationist protégé of the powerful Talmadge clan, and although I deplored his election, I felt oddly compelled to attend the ceremony.

I couldn't persuade any of my friends to go, so I went alone. I stood on the edge of the crowd of 1,000 or more people milling around on the capitol grounds. All eyes turned toward the dignitaries and their wives who were filling the speakers' platform at the top of the high front entrance steps. The governors of Alabama, South Carolina, Florida, and Tennessee were all present, a row of pompous males arranged like so many clay pigeons at a shooting gallery.

The admiring, cheering crowd was 100 percent white. Although the capitol is within walking distance of a large black residential area, I did not see a single black person. The visiting governors delivered meaningless, hate-filled speeches, as if each one were trying to prove that he was more of a segregationist die-hard than the previous speaker. The crowd cheered wildly after each speech. The Rebel yells were so loud they could be heard all the way to Peachtree Street, half a mile from the capitol.

The band played. The cannon on the lawn boomed out its salute to the new governor. The audience applauded and cheered more. I felt sad and forlorn. I remember thinking, "Go ahead, Governor Vandiver, say anything you want to, but I know better. Black kids will go to school with white kids, and they will receive a more nearly equal education. My friends and I will help them. We will be like David to your Goliath."

The state legislature, in the face of a Supreme Court mandate to come up with a plan, could reach no agreement. After much fiery debate, the state senate and assembly began talking about closing all the schools in Georgia rather than integrate them. At this point the "No, not one" rhetoric began in earnest.

It was demagoguery at its worst, led by our two U.S. senators, Richard B. Russell and Herman Talmadge. With their sanction, it filtered down and became even more heated with the county court-house crowd, especially those seeking office. Each speaker tried to be more "nigger hating" than his opponent.

A little more than a year later, in March of 1958, I was elected president of the Atlanta League. I served a two-year term. Those two years were worth more to me than a degree in political science. Virtually every issue that we studied in order to educate the public had racial overtones, especially education. The League helped persuade the Atlanta school board to adopt a desegregation policy, and we were adamant that funds should be more equitably distributed among white and black schools.

At about this time I hired a maid named Dorothy. Throughout World War II, Dorothy had worked in Washington as a stenographer, but when the war ended she was laid off and returned to Atlanta, her family's home. Not surprisingly, Dorothy couldn't find a job here as a stenographer, although she was obviously well qualified. So she turned to domestic work.

When I found out that Dorothy could type, I was delighted, because the League assignments with which I was involved required typed reports. Since I wasn't a good typist, I made a deal with Dorothy. She would use my typewriter to type up reports while I did the house-work! It was a very helpful arrangement for me, but Dorothy was both efficient and reliable, and with my recommendation she soon got a job as a secretary for one of Atlanta's schools. It was work far more suited to her skills and much more profitable than the going household clean-ing wage of about ten dollars a week.

My League involvement led me to become an official observer at Atlanta school board meetings. For roughly three years, I attended practically every monthly meeting. So I came to know the personalities, see what needed to get done, and understand the way decisions were made. I saw what I'd want to change, especially in terms of racial equality. I got my political education all because of the League. It was, and forty years later still is, the perfect training ground for any woman interested in politics, especially one who might be thinking about running for office herself.

In the mid to late 1950s, it became more and more obvious that the Supreme Court's 1954 ruling in *Brown v. Board of Education* would need to be implemented by the federal government throughout the South, and possibly with force, as we had seen in Little Rock, at the University of Alabama, and in other places.

But the likelihood of federal intervention didn't keep die-hard racist southern politicians from spouting off as they had at the inauguration of Governor Ernest Vandiver. In 1957, B. D. (Buck) Murphy, a Georgia legislator and lawyer, was quoted in the *Atlanta Constitution* as saying, "There will be no integration in schools, in churches, in colleges in my lifetime or yours. No social, political, economic or military power is sufficient to bring it about."

Southern lawyers were paid millions of dollars to circumvent the law that could no longer be used as an excuse for segregated schools. The new law, however, had a basic flaw. It commanded not that segregation end at once but that the end should be effected "with all deliberate speed." "All deliberate speed" proved open to a wide range of interpretations.

The lawlessness of the Old West scarcely exceeded that in the South before and after 1954. Whatever the cost to the taxpayer of the Civil War of 1861–1865, it cannot have matched the amount spent in the futile effort to maintain segregation.

An editorial in the *Atlanta Constitution* observed, "The fact is that state government played a major role in resistance to school desegregation in Georgia, and local school systems are continuing to pay a price for outright defiance of the law and foot-dragging they engaged in with the state's encouragement." Chatham County (Savannah) ran up a bill of $28 million to eliminate the schools' dual system.

After 1954 southern lawyers were paid more millions to "circumvent" the civil rights laws or, if this was not possible, to see that litigation in the courts stalled change for years. The eventual victory for civil rights is now history. The first few token blacks to attend a white school in Atlanta did so in 1961, seven years after the 1954 ruling supposedly ended segregated schools in the South.

A lawyer friend told me, "In some areas huge fees were paid to favored [segregationist] lawyers to delay the Supreme Court decisions. I suppose the pay is less if you conciliate and more if you litigate."

In addition to the highly paid lawyers, school administrators and local school boards in the South (which consisted 99 percent of white males) were frantically trying to find any and all means, whether legal or illegal, to stop, or at least delay, integration for as long as possible.

A lawyer friend in Texas wrote me in 1963 that he had heard the attorney general of a southern state tell a group of lawyers, "He and they knew the Supreme Court's rulings were binding, but he would not so admit publicly as he felt it was lawyers' duty to delay and postpone. This seems to be the attitude of so many school board lawyers in Georgia, Texas, and other Confederate states."

Despite the best efforts of politicians, a raft of states'-rights segregationist organizations, and their lawyers, pressure from the federal government led the state legislature to set up a commission to determine whether the citizens of Georgia wanted to close the public schools or keep them open and integrate them. John Sibley, a prominent Atlanta lawyer, was named chairman.

The Sibley Commission, as it came to be known, held ten standing-room-only hearings throughout the state in 1960. The main purpose, as it turned out, was to give angry white citizens a chance to vent their wrath. In addition, the hearings made people face reality. For three days I attended the hearings in Atlanta as a representative of the League of Women Voters. The League of course favored keeping the schools open at all costs. All of the League's dissenting members had resigned at our infamous 1956 annual meeting. While I waited for my turn to speak before the commission, I noticed how the sunlight coming through the high, dirty windows of Henry Grady High School's gym caught the blond hair of a three-year-old peacefully sleeping on his mother's lap. I figured he was the most important person in that big building. It was his future we were debating as well as the future of Georgia.

When it came time for me to step up to the microphone, I said, "I am Sara Mitchell, a native Georgian who came today to represent the Atlanta League of Women Voters. The League is opposed to the closing of our public schools. If they are closed, what national companies will open offices here? Georgia will suffer irreparable damage to its image, its history, and its people."

The final report from the Sibley Commission was published in 1961, while I was campaigning for election to the school board. The majority report was signed by eleven members who wanted to keep the schools open and also wanted to control any form of integration decreed by the federal courts. The minority agreed: "We deplore the Supreme Court decision to integrate the public schools; at the same time we recognize it is now the law, and that Georgia must cope with it in some way."

The minority report was signed by eight members who wanted to "keep the present segregation laws and close all the schools if the court ordered any integration anywhere, anytime." The eight further stated, "The minority of commissioners deplore and condemn efforts on the part of 'Communist' inspired organizations to legalize integration, and thus inflict incalculable damage to the welfare and future happiness of this state."

"Communist inspired"! How many times did I hear the phrase in those days? The label was applied to every decent, law-abiding organization to which I belonged, regardless of any connection with the

Communist Party. Indeed, I never saw any such connection during the almost two decades I worked for the civil rights movement.

The Sibley Commission report stated that "1,800 witnesses (1,600 white and 200 blacks), representing 115,000 citizens in the state, testified. Two out of three favored closing the schools rather than comply with the orders from the Supreme Court."

Such was the general picture in 1961. Public education in Atlanta in 1961 was marred by bitterness, strife, and uncertainty. The prospect afforded little ground for hope. In fact that year, the Board of Education finally came up with a plan to comply with *Brown v. Board of Education.* Upon closer inspection, however, the plan merely paid lip service to the notion of compliance.

The board's plan provided for integrating schools one grade at a time, beginning with the twelfth grade. A full year later, the eleventh grade would be integrated, and so on, until finally kindergarten would be integrated—more than a decade later! Even in the South, noted for being slow to change, this plan was ridiculous.

Under the plan, any black student who wanted to transfer to a white school had to pick up an application form, take an aptitude and assessment test, and submit to a personal interview. One hundred and thirty-three black students submitted requests for transfer. Out of these, only ten students who were outstanding in character, academic achievement, and ability were selected to attend the senior class of five white schools. As with Noah's ark, they were to go two by two. The final day of reckoning, the day Atlanta's public schools opened, was August 30, 1961. School desegregation was occurring just as the campaigns for local offices were getting underway. I was therefore especially anxious to see what was about to unfold.

I awoke on the morning of August 30 tense and apprehensive. I turned on my bedside radio right away. The local announcer reporting on the opening of the schools sounded like Edward R. Murrow, the famous World War II correspondent, as he reported the bombing of London by the Nazis. Public officials had urged Atlantans who did not have to go to work to stay at home. Under no circumstances was anyone to go as an onlooker to any of the five schools that were being integrated.

The City Council's chamber had been converted into a vast pressroom. A dozen television sets showed each school and the two black students as they were entering. Direct radio contact and an open, amplified two-way telephone setup provided reporters with coverage of the news as it happened. I tried to visualize the scene: police stationed around the high schools, police dogs straining at leashes, held tight but ready in a split second to be released. As I listened I felt ashamed for our town, sorrow for the scared black students and their frightened parents, and disappointment for all of us white southerners. What were the white students in these high schools feeling and thinking, I wondered? What were black parents all over town, and black students, thinking and feeling as they listened to their radios or watched on television?

Amazingly, there were no demonstrations and no violence. There was no Ku Klux Klan march. The "plan" prevented mobs of white parents and onlookers from ringing the school grounds shouting racial epithets, as they had in Little Rock, Arkansas, four years earlier.

In fact, Atlanta received national recognition for desegregating without disorder. Congratulations poured in. President Kennedy personally contacted Governor Ernest Vandiver, who had publicly declared that no black child would ever attend school with a white child in Georgia.

President Kennedy also congratulated school superintendent John Letson and all parents, students, and citizens for "the law-abiding manner in which the five high schools were desegregated today. I strongly urge the officials and citizens of all communities that face this difficult transition in the coming weeks and months to look closely at what Atlanta and Georgia have done—with courage, tolerance and, above all, with respect to the law."

The Atlanta school staff even congratulated itself. "It is a story of astute and courageous leadership by public officials, of unremitting and responsible presentation of all the facts by the press, of dispassionate and free discussion of issues by religious and lay organizations and a hard-nosed, no-foolishness attitude on the part of the police department."

All this self-congratulation in the media proved too much for the black community to swallow. The *Atlanta Daily World,* the city's leading black newspaper, published an editorial stating: "Nobody does us a favor when he grudgingly doles out to us a fraction of our rights. Atlanta must turn away from the congratulations and autograph parties and come to grips with the terrible inequalities that are crippling thousands of our innocent children. This can never be done in a stifling atmosphere of Hear No Evil, See No Evil, Speak No Evil."

Shortly thereafter many human problems surfaced. One of the transfer students, for example, withdrew from Northside High even though she was academically outstanding. She explained that the tension and stress of all the publicity resulted in an unbearable situation. "I am constantly in the limelight. . . . if there were more Negro students, I might feel the loss of former classmates less, and the burden of loneliness I feel at Northside would be lighter." At a meeting of the Greater Atlanta Human Rights Council the following question was raised: "Would it be possible to designate a particularly sympathetic, friendly teacher in each of the five schools to act as an advisor?" What a sad commentary it seemed that many white teachers didn't volunteer for such an assignment.

Remarkably enough, virtually all the transfer students held up well under the terrible daily pressure. One of the female students who integrated Murphy High (on the poor white south side of town) surely deserved a medal. I heard her tell a group of sympathetic white adults this story:

"I was walking down the hall between classes, late for the next one. The hall was empty except for a group of five white boys who came walking slowly and ominously toward me. One look at them and I tensed up. I could tell by the way they walked, by the cold look in their eyes that something premeditated and threatening was about to happen. When they got right up to me one of them pulled something from inside his football jacket and stuck it right in my face—a white rat they had taken from the science lab. My heart was pounding but I managed to stay pretty calm. . . . I took the rat from him gently and cuddled it in my hands. I looked at them and said, 'Isn't he beautiful?' Then I gave it back and walked away."

Another student, now Madelyn Nix-Beamen, a corporate lawyer in Pennsylvania, remembers a lonely year at Brown High "when no more than three white students ever acted friendly towards me." Nix-Beamen also recalled childish pranks by white boys, who "splashed Coca-Cola on my white dress. None of that turned me away, but only strengthened my sense of humor and my need to press on. We as a race have incredible coping skills, and that's what helped to get me through."

Still another transfer student, Martha Ann Holmes-Jackson, now a third grade teacher in the Atlanta school system, said of a recent anniversary of the day schools opened in 1961, "It will be just another day. But I will think back on what we did and the progress we made for our race. . . . I will smile, maybe just a little brighter."

When the city took its woefully inadequate first step toward school integration in August 1961, I was running for a place on the Board of Education. Several factors had contributed to my decision to run— my involvement with the League of Women Voters, my faith in my ability to help make Atlanta's public schools better, and my convictions as a Christian. But most important was my friendship with many blacks in those early days of the civil rights movement. I knew I could help, especially with the transition as Atlanta's public schools were integrated. The trick was to get elected.

I was keenly aware that the campaign entailed plenty of challenges. First, I knew I needed money. The entrance fee alone for the Board of Education was set at $900. How would I get the large campaign committee I would need? Would I have the stamina to speak at months of rallies and to shake thousands of hands? Could I walk a tightrope, appealing to "moderate" whites and at the same time to virtually every black voter in the city?

I spent many sleepless nights thinking it over. My primary worry was my husband. He had become increasingly unhappy about my public life. He said things like "Why don't you have coffee with the neighbors' wives, play bridge, and go out to lunch like all my friends' wives?"

I put off talking with Ray about my desire to seek office because I knew he wouldn't approve. Increasingly, however, I felt confidence in my ability to do things without Ray's sanction. The trouble was that in this instance I couldn't go ahead without his money.

Any money at our house was always "his" money. During the first twenty years of our marriage, I never had access to a checking account—mine, ours, or even his. Ray gave me a household "allowance," like a child. Every time I wanted a dress or anything else that cost more than about fifty dollars, I had to make a special request—humiliating then and even more so when I look back on it today.

For this very special request, I chose as favorable a time as I could. I approached Ray after I had cooked him a nice dinner. I said, "Some wives whose husbands are in your income bracket ask for expensive jewelry or a mink coat. What I want is $1,000 to run for the Board of Education."

Ray stared at me in shock. Before he could recover, I played my trump card: "If I'm elected, the salary is $200 a month for four years, which amounts to $9,600. So I'll be able to pay you the $1,000 back." On these terms, seeing my determination, Ray agreed. Neither of us acknowledged the possibility that I might not win.

As soon as word started getting out that I was seriously considering running, I began to get telephone calls. One of the first came from Jerry Reed, Dr. King's white dentist. "I hear you're thinking about running for a seat on the school board from our ward. If you decide against it, how about letting me know? I'm thinking of running myself, but there's no sense in us two liberals splitting the vote." I promised to let Jerry know by the next afternoon.

The next day was a dismal, rainy Sunday. I lay on the bed watching fat raindrops slide down the windowpane. The phone was beside me. I knew I had to make up my mind one way or the other. I did not hear any voices telling me what to do, but suddenly I recalled something I had read by the German philosopher Nietzsche: "Not to win, that's not a sin—the sin comes from not trying." I called Jerry and told him I was going to give it a shot. He was kind enough to say, "Sara, from the tone of your voice, I have the feeling you're going to win. Good luck!"

3

Running Scared for Public Office

When I decided to run for office I had no real idea of what I was getting into, so I had to learn fast. I got plenty of advice from friends who had been candidates. I was overwhelmed by the task as they described it. The best advice I got was to take one day at a time.

I was particularly lucky to have Helen Bullard, Atlanta's political public relations maven, as a friend. Helen had managed Mayor William B. Hartsfield's three successful campaigns, so I called and asked her to lunch. Before the appetizers arrived, I blurted out, "Helen, do you think I could get elected to the Atlanta school board? What are my chances?"

Helen had a slow, soft way of speaking. "Well," she said, "I don't know. You look too much the southern lady. The public won't respond or relate to you—except those in your own little social, volunteer-work world. How many people do you know? How long is your Christmas card list? If you wrote down every person you and your husband know, you probably couldn't come up with 1,000 names."

I knew she was right, and I was worried.

Helen did offer me a ray of hope, however. "You have a good last name—Mitchell. That won't turn anyone off." Then came the punch line: "Now if your first name were Margaret, you'd have it made!" She added, "If you're really serious, come by my office and I'll design a handout card for you to give to people at campaign rallies. And I'll also see that you have a good photographer."

But my first visit for that head shot proved a disaster. I took the proofs to Helen. She wailed, "These are horrible!" Dialing the photographer, she said, "Why is it that when I send you a pot-bellied, cigar-smoking male candidate, your photos make him look like the president of Yale University? For once I send you nice, ladylike Mrs. Mitchell, and you send shots back that make her look like a matron in a juvenile detention center. I'm sending her back over there right now."

I felt sorry for the photographer and tried to explain to Helen that I always took a lousy picture. But the second round did look better.

Just the opposite proved true of my main opponent in the race, a businessman named Dan MacIntyre. He was one of the best-looking men I ever saw. His campaign photos made him look like Cary Grant's double.

True to her word, Helen soon had the card designed and printed. It was two by three inches, with blue type on white stock. It read, "We need a Qualified, Dedicated, Experienced, Capable Woman on the Atlanta Board of Education. Elect Mrs. Ray Mitchell, 8th Ward." A head shot of me was there, too. I felt encouraged and impressed.

The handout card read: "Qualified . . . Dedicated . . . Experienced . . . Capable . . . Woman." Not one of these words in any way alluded to my liberal, integrationist beliefs, and the omission was a hard political reality I had to face right away. If I had come out and said I was for integrating the public schools of Atlanta immediately because every child deserved the same education regardless of his or her skin color, I could just as well have burned the $1,000 I had borrowed from my husband.

Indeed, there was no way, given the racial turmoil that was building in the spring of 1961, that anyone, white or black, could have been elected on such a platform in Atlanta in a citywide race. And yet, as you'll see, I did get my views out, even if I had to do it quietly.

In my official campaign bio press release, for instance, the last quoted statement read: "In the approaching transition period of At-

lanta's schools, I will work in harmony with the school superintendent, the school board and the school administration." Not exactly
fiery rhetoric, but by merely acknowledging the coming of some kind
of integration and saying I would work in "harmony" with everyone,
I was taking a stronger stance than you might think today.

Elizabeth Gilette, a friend of mine and a former board member in
the League of Women Voters, called and volunteered to be my campaign manager. I felt immense relief. Elizabeth proved to be a whiz at
organizing, and she didn't waste any time. The first thing she said was,
"We need a copy of the Voters' Registration List for the City of Atlanta." When I discovered that the list would cost $100, I told her I
couldn't afford it. She was adamant, so I figured I might as well spend
the $100 I had left over after paying the $900 entrance fee.

We planned a big "morning coffee" at my house to kick off my campaign. The black women who had become friends at civil rights and
League meetings volunteered to campaign for me in their wards. That
led to a hard decision in 1961. Could I invite them to meet with my
white friends? I needed my white friends as workers because of their
church, PTA, and club connections. Most of them had never met with
blacks as social equals at someone's home. Still, I could not run an
honest race based on a platform of equality and integration unless I
did invite them, so I went ahead.

At my house, then, a group of upper-middle-class, Northside Atlanta women sat down socially with blacks for the first time. They later
told me that the experience had been an exciting event in their lives
and that they were happy to have taken part in it. From this point
onward, my campaign was off to a good start. The volunteers amazed
me with all their help. They made thousands of phone calls and sent
out hundreds of letters and cards. The most valuable, interesting,
stimulating, rewarding years of my life began with this campaign, one
of the first truly integrated campaigns in Atlanta's history.

Longtime mayor William B. Hartsfield had decided not to seek reelection. My friend Helen Bullard was now managing the campaign

for prominent businessman Ivan Allen, but as busy as she was, she still volunteered her time to advise me on how to spend the campaign contributions I began to receive. This too was an amazing experience. With only a brief letter from my campaign treasurer, money began to come in. I received a contribution of seventy-five dollars—then a large amount—from an Episcopal priest I had never met. Other donations came from people who later told me, "I gave because you represent how I feel about the race problem." In the 1990s, $4,000 seems a small amount to have raised, but in the early 1960s it was a windfall.

When I had enough funds to cover the campaign's immediate needs, I called Helen for advice. She thought for a second, then said she had secured a half hour on Atlanta's most popular television station the next week for Ivan Allen. She would see if she could buy me the following fifteen minutes. I asked, "What in the world will I say or do for a whole fifteen minutes?" "That's no problem," she said. "Get your husband to say what a fine wife and mother you are, then get your minister to praise you as a good Sunday school teacher and churchgoer."

Amazingly, Ray agreed. He was handsome and had a clear, polished voice and the demeanor of an executive. He did a very good job and came across well. Dr. Nat G. Long, my longtime minister, praised me more than I deserved. He had gone with me to that 1947 integrated political rally.

The very first rally for all the candidates was held in a downtown black Baptist church. I arrived on time only to find the other candidates already there, working the crowd. It hadn't crossed my mind to bring anyone with me, since the meeting was being held at a black church. Ray certainly wasn't a prospect. I entered the church alone and primly took a seat down front.

When my turn came to speak, I read the few lines I had written on three-by-five cards in a small, scared voice that was much too low for the church's high ceilings. My two college courses in public speaking, my leadership in the League, and my years of Sunday school teaching did not stand me in good stead. After the rally Lonnie King, a prominent black civil rights activist, took me aside. "I want you to win," he said, "but there's something you have to learn or your campaign will be in trouble on this side of town. You don't pronounce Negro the way it should be pronounced. Say KNEE-GROW. Keep practicing until you get it perfect." Like virtually all southern whites, I had grown up pronouncing the word more like "nei-gra."

Some weeks later speaking at another rally in a black neighborhood, I had a sudden inspiration. Forgetting my cards and my set speech, I told the audience about the time I attended probably the first integrated political rally ever in Atlanta fourteen years earlier, in 1947. My story of that gathering in the Wheat Street Baptist Church got the rapt attention of the audience and even my fellow candidates. The timekeeper forgot to call time when my allotted three minutes were up. From that night onward, I felt truly accepted by Atlanta's black community.

There was a rally almost every night during that long, hot summer of 1961 and often two or three. Sam Massell, who was running for vice mayor, told me his secretary kept records. Before the summer was even over, there had already been fifty-eight rallies. I don't think I missed more than three or four.

At each one I introduced myself, listed my qualifications, and promised to work for better, equal educational opportunities for all students. The key words were "equal" and "all." In the 1960s, black neighborhoods were very close knit, so whether you were "for or against us" was well known before you got up to speak. I felt the people at the rallies just wanted to look us in the eye and decide for themselves whether as candidates we were sincere, which meant whether we were truly for integration, although the word was never used outright.

Although the race was nonpartisan, it was no secret that the Republican Party had asked Dan MacIntyre to run. The Republicans were anxious to support candidates who would later become well known and win higher office. As many times as I heard Dan's three-minute speech, I don't recall anything he ever said. As for Mrs. Ragsdale, the incumbent, I was convinced that some school administrator had written her speech. She carefully read from three-by-five cards, and neither the message nor her intonation ever varied one iota. Actually, I didn't hear her very often, because Mrs. Ragsdale didn't come to any rallies in black neighborhoods—and rallies in black neighborhoods accounted for about 90 percent of all such events.

In addition to attending rallies, my chief responsibility as a candidate was to see as many people as possible who could influence voters. I tried not to miss a single lead. For example, if someone told me, "The corner druggist in West End knows everyone out there. Go see him," I went.

One of the strangest encounters came after a friend told me, "Be sure to see Mrs. Geneva Haugabrooks." Mrs. Haugabrooks was the black owner of Haugabrooks' Undertaking Parlor, which was down one block from Ebenezer Baptist Church and diagonally across from Wheat Street Baptist—in other words, right in the heart of the black community.

I arrived one afternoon at about two o'clock, walked across the porch floor, which had been freshly painted, and knocked on the door. A tall, thin black man impeccably dressed in a dark suit and a starched white shirt opened the door and stared at me. I told him I would like to see Mrs. Haugabrooks. In a deep, solemn voice he said, "Wait in the sitting room." I sat down in the sparsely furnished room and waited. My eyes focused on the highly polished, bare floors and the white walls with their colorful prints of religious subjects.

After a few minutes the man returned and motioned for me to follow him down a long, narrow central hall to the rear of the house. He slowly opened one of the doors and announced in his deep baritone, "Mrs. Haugabrooks will see you now." Peering into the darkened room, I saw Mrs. Haugabrooks lying down on one of the laying-in beds used for viewing. She was apparently taking her afternoon nap. From the direction of the bed I heard a sweet, far-off, serene voice say, "Come over here, dear, and sit by me. What can I do for you?"

I found a chair near her, sat down, and tried to collect my wits. Despite the macabre setting, I managed somehow to explain my platform. I was arguing that Atlanta schools should concentrate, not on sports and time-consuming extracurricular activities, but on the basics—reading, writing, and arithmetic. I also assured her I would speak up for improved, equal education for *all* students.

Mrs. Haugabrooks and I then proceeded to have a lengthy, satisfying conversation about the issues involved, especially the urgent need for better educational opportunities for black students. Although my visit had been unannounced, she showed great poise, which I admired, as well as considerable knowledge of the city's politics. Before my visit was over I had won her support. It later proved to be very helpful. Mrs. Haugabrooks was respected by hundreds and hundreds of people.

Four decades ago political candidates got questionnaires from lots of civic organizations just as they do today. And by 1961 many black organizations had produced questionnaires like the following, from the Atlanta Negro Voters League, dated August 7, 1961. My answers, as best as I can recall them, appear in italics following each question:

The Atlanta Negro Voters League is inviting all candidates who are seeking public office in the September 13 Primary Election to meet with its Executive Committee, and other leaders, at the Butler Street YMCA, Room 4, on August 10th, 11th and 12th, 1961. At this time, each candidate will have an opportunity to present his background and platform, and give his views on the issues that are listed below.

The candidates for Mayor will have fifteen minutes each to present their cases, while those for the Board of Aldermen and Board of Education will have ten minutes each.

Questions to Candidates for the Board of Education

1. Will you vigorously and continuously work to have the Board of Education comply with the Supreme Court decisions of 1954, and to eliminate the unnecessary, complicated series of applications for admission required, and thereby hasten the democratization of Atlanta's schools?

Yes, definitely. One of my primary goals is to seek improved, equal education for ALL students—and this should be accomplished quickly, with a minimum of bureaucratic delay.

2. Would you present, or support, a resolution or policy statement of the Board of Education specifying non-discriminatory clauses in all School Construction Contracts?

Yes, but at the same time I also support consideration of the Board's low-bid policy.

3. Would you support a resolution restricting employment in school construction work to residents in Metropolitan Atlanta?

Yes, as long as we maintain a sufficient number of well-qualified employees in the city.

4. Would you support the immediate establishment of a first class area vocational school in Atlanta, staffed by technically trained personnel without regard to race?

Yes, I am in agreement with the present Board and school administration that this is a high priority.

5. Will you vigorously and continually work to improve the quality of the educational program of the Atlanta Public Schools, with especial reference to bringing student test performance up to the national midpoint, or the 50th percentile, as an immediate goal?

Absolutely. As your members hopefully know by this point in the campaign, one of my core beliefs is that the Board should do everything in its power to emphasize the basics of education—reading, writing and arithmetic—instead of expensive athletic programs and other unnecessary extra-curricular activities.

At the end of questionnaires like these, and after rallies, I usually said, "I believe we should have a woman on the Board of Education whose children are products of the Atlanta schools, and I believe we should have a person who has worked actively with the PTA."

As a rule, the majority of our rallies in the black section of town were sponsored by small civic organizations. Before a rally, these groups usually printed up a sheet listing the candidates who had won their endorsement. These "tickets" were all-important, so I would pick up one and scan it for my name as soon as I arrived. One night I noticed that the Southside Civic Club had endorsed Dan MacIntyre, my opponent. I was stunned, since this was the first endorsement I had failed to receive from a black organization.

When my time came to speak to the group, I walked up to the podium and gave the civic club and guests a fiery, indignant dressing down. "I can't believe my eyes. My opponent has never given any indication that he will be as supportive to your interests as I will. Why did I fail to get your endorsement? If you don't vote for me, you'll regret it."

I was surprised by my own outburst, and so was the audience. The long, hot summer of campaigning was beginning to take its toll. Dan of course sat there looking as pleased as I was upset. I believe this was the only endorsement he received from a black group, and unfortunately for him the Southside Civic Club didn't speak for many voters. I won the district's vote by a large majority.

At our rallies, the tension and controversy among competing office-seekers created an undercurrent of excitement. I soon learned which of the forty-odd candidates supported me and which opposed me. Rumors and gossip flew back and forth each night, but the candidates were mostly a friendly group. We would stand outside on the steps of the church or hall where we were appearing, laughing and talking until our turn came to speak.

About three weeks before the primary and just one week before the city's schools were desegregated, I got great coverage in several newspaper articles, as this excerpt from the September 8, 1961, *Atlanta Constitution* shows:

> This soft-spoken candidate knows what she believes. And it's basically that she has both the school and political background to do an intelligent job.
>
> She worked her way through almost all PTA offices as her three children progressed through Atlanta public schools. Her League background covers 10 years of almost every field of civic investigation, including heading its education committee. She is immediate past president.
>
> But more than background, Mrs. Mitchell thinks the voters want to know what she believes. Basically, it is that Atlanta schools need
>
> 1. A return to basic education—less social, recreational and spiritual emphasis and more straight academics.
>
> 2. More "depth" in the teaching of vital subjects like English, math, history, science and languages.
>
> 3. More respect and prestige for teachers. "I can't make any campaign promises," she says, "because I believe in weighing each issue as it arises. It's the ability to handle the unforeseen, the unexpected, that's important."

In general, these articles stressed my personal qualifications: they noted that I was a mother, a wife, and active in civic and church organizations. One included a large photo of me with my daughter Susan and her first child. None of these write-ups mentioned "integration" directly, but as I've said, there were code words such as "all," "equal," "change," and "improve," and everyone could read between the lines.

I'm sorry that my core integrationist beliefs were not mentioned in the Atlanta papers. If they had been, though, I would certainly have been branded a "radical" at a tense time when moderate voters were looking for leaders who exuded calm, reason, and reassurance. We liberals wanted to make voters think, not to upset them.

Seven candidates were vying for the city's top job, but there were really only two main contenders: Ivan Allen, a prominent, respected, moderate businessman, and Lester Maddox, a blustery, bantamweight, bigoted restaurant owner.

Maddox was known for having refused to serve blacks in his tourist eatery, The Pickrick. He sold pickricks, or ax handles, that he had personally autographed. Somehow these stood for the right to defend one's person and property against uppity outside black agitators whose goal was the annihilation of the southern way of life. I sat next to Maddox on the podium at campaign rallies on many occasions. He knew where I stood on segregation, so we would greet each other politely, then look quickly away.

Lester's views made him a shoo-in to garner the segregationist vote, but even in 1961 he needed more. Blacks had registered to vote and had organized enough to hold the balance of power. No politician in a citywide race could win without at least some votes of the opposite race. Although black voters were fewer in number than white voters, blacks voted much more monolithically. In practical terms, a moderate white candidate had to get virtually 100 percent of the black vote plus 15 percent of the white vote—and that's about what the percentage of liberal-to-moderate white voters in Atlanta was at the time.

My Board of Education race was mild and insignificant by comparison with the more important contests. As the September primary neared, the campaign was getting hotter than the stifling weather. By long tradition the final rally was held at the black Wheat Street Baptist Church the night before the election. The large sanctuary began filling an hour before the announced time. Tonight was to be the end-all showdown.

Appearing first were the seven contenders for mayor. Ivan Allen was the front-runner. Lester Maddox didn't seem to have a chance, since he could only count on votes from segregationist die-hards—or at least that's what the blacks and white liberals hoped. (There were enough segregationist voters throughout the state of Georgia to put Maddox in the governor's seat five years later, I'm sorry to say.)

"Muggsy" Smith, one of the other candidates for mayor, was a well-liked, hardworking state legislator from Fulton County. That night he entered the church late with a large delegation of his black supporters, all of whom must have realized by now that they had backed a loser. When his turn came to speak, he proceeded to whip his followers into an emotional frenzy. He claimed to be the most "liberal tiger in the jungle." Muggsy's desperate attempt to win the primary proved embarrassing to his friends and supporters. He had always been known as a nice guy. For some reason no one ever understood, he completely blew his cool that preelection night and with it any chance he might have had to win. The other four candidates for mayor were also-rans. I recall one whose only campaign issue was synchronizing all the traffic lights on Peachtree Street.

At this last rally I felt confident, maybe even a little cocky, concerning my chances of winning. I sat back cool and calm while awaiting my turn to speak. My three minutes at the podium didn't come until nearly midnight, and they were surely an anticlimax in the most racially charged city campaign yet held in Atlanta. I simply repeated my usual remarks but perhaps with more vigor. Election Day came as a relief. Finally there was nothing more any candidate could do. I voted, then went over to see a good friend. We spoke of subjects other than politics and campaigning. I don't recall being agitated or worried about the outcome of the election.

Back in September of 1961, there wasn't really any local exit polling, so you just sat and waited for the precinct-by-precinct vote tallies to be recorded by City Hall and announced over television and radio. My campaign committee felt very good about my chances, primarily because of my strength in the black community but also because I had not openly offended the white community. Furthermore, neither of my opponents had played any kind of race card. The incumbent, Mrs. Clifford Ragsdale, had done little active campaigning, so we didn't think she posed much of a threat.

Feeling calm and confident, I fixed Ray and myself an early supper, then got hors d'oeuvres ready for about eight members of my campaign committee. Anticipating a victory at the polls, we thought watching the returns together would make for a happy evening, especially when the victory champagne was served. I completely failed to anticipate the emotional roller coaster of the next few hours.

Starting at seven, right when the polls closed, all three of Atlanta's network affiliates devoted the entire night to coverage of the returns. The results, especially for mayor, were very eagerly awaited. Soon the big studio scoreboards began showing early returns. We stayed with WSB, the oldest, most respected station in town.

To our horror, the first returns on WSB showed Dan MacIntyre ahead by several thousand votes, and the next ones had his lead increasing by another 4,000. We were stunned. I began to go to pieces. Helen Bullard, my unofficial campaign guru, had told me months ago that you could tell the outcome of an election from the reports of the first fourteen precincts. Well, twenty precincts had reported, and each set of returns showed MacIntyre increasing his lead by thousands of votes.

Then an amazing thing happened. WSB's anchorman said, "Over in the race for the Board of Education, there seems to be a mix-up. . . . through some kind of technical error, the vote tally for Mitchell and MacIntyre has been switched. *Mitchell* is in fact running ahead by more than 10,000 votes, not MacIntyre." We screamed with relief and joy. In a few seconds I catapulted from despair to heady elation—which is fine for roller coaster riders but not for a novice political candidate. My lead continued to build until all the votes were in, late that night. I won six of the city's eight wards (districts) and amassed almost 6,000 votes more than Dan MacIntyre.

But the roller coaster high was also short-lived, because although

Mrs. Ragsdale had come in a poor third, she had, simply by virtue of being the incumbent, garnered enough votes to force MacIntyre and me into a runoff, to be held just eight days later. The top two mayoral candidates, moderate Ivan Allen and segregationist Lester Maddox, were also in the runoff, as were several other candidates for alderman. The runoff was sure to generate a high turnout.

When I realized I'd have to start campaigning again, ask for more money, go to more rallies, and do it all in one week, I went into an emotional tailspin. I was not happy about the prospect of another race. I felt tired and drained. We had spent our last campaign dollar. My committee thought I had come out well, but we decided to save the champagne.

The next morning was a miserable day. I burrowed deep under the covers, not wanting to face the world. Soon the phone began ringing. League members and other friends called to tell me how thrilled they were. Although my spirits were low, the offers to send more money did help. In the remaining days before the runoff, I had more volunteer help, more contributions, and more free television exposure than I could have hoped for.

The main forum came on the eve of the runoff. Dan MacIntyre and I (the only two school board candidates in a runoff) participated in a one-hour telecast with the vice mayoral candidates and several alderman hopefuls. For some reason Ivan Allen and Lester Maddox were not on the air. The *Atlanta Constitution* for September 22, 1961, reported the debate.

According to the article, "both Massell and Evans, the vice mayor candidates, admitted they wanted both Negro and white support during Friday's election, but Evans said, 'I do not know how I will fare. I do not honestly see how the Negro citizens could vote against me as a bloc. I have done many things to help them.'"

Asked what we considered "the most pressing problem" facing Atlanta education today, MacIntyre reportedly said, "I have only one campaign promise: to do my utmost to give each child the best possible education." I called "a terrible overcrowding" in the public schools

the top problem, with "too many children in too few classrooms."
MacIntyre and I disagreed on the question of federal aid to education.
I said, "Anyone interested in education would certainly accept the
funds." MacIntyre said, "We do not need to have federal aid. We should
seek state money first."

It was now September of 1961. Our city's schools had just been integrated, albeit barely so, and none of the participants in the election-
eve broadcast, myself included, even mentioned the fact. Looking
back, I find the omission inconceivable. Maybe the reporter didn't
think the subject important enough to write about. Or maybe the
moderator never asked us about it. Could we all have been too scared
to mention the issue ourselves? Was it too loaded a topic?

Although desegregation is not mentioned explicitly, the article in
a couple of places hints at the subject. First, the statement "both
Massell and Evans admitted they wanted both Negro and white support" suggests that it would have been possible for one or both candidates to do otherwise. What mainstream candidate running for *anything* today wouldn't claim to want the support of voters of all races?

There's another hint of racial tension. I'm quoted as being in favor
of federal aid to education and MacIntyre as opposing it. In that day,
"federal aid" was clearly understood to mean integration, because of
course the federal government was compelling local school districts
to comply with the Supreme Court's *Brown v. Board of Education* ruling.
Our stances on federal aid told every television viewer and newspaper
reader where MacIntyre and I stood on integration. MacIntyre was
trying to appeal to as many white voters as possible, because it was
clear from the first election that I was going to get all the black vote.

The silence that we candidates maintained about race shows just
how different, unsettled, uncharted, and even scary a time it was
for Atlantans. Our hallowed way of life was being challenged, criticized, and literally outlawed by infamous "outside agitators"—most
of whom were actually elected federal officials and members of our
nation's highest court.

The runoff gave me no roller coaster ride, thank goodness! I not only handily beat MacIntyre by nearly 20,000 votes but also won more votes than any candidate except Ivan Allen, who crushed segregationist Lester Maddox, much to the relief of every right-thinking Atlantan.

My home phone soon began to ring off the hook with congratulations from well-wishers. Calls came from the three major television stations inviting me to come down to their studios and thank my voters. Since it was late, Ray agreed to go with me. I think he was stunned by my victory, never having really believed I would win. I admit I enjoyed all the calls, all the attention. I liked being on television, and Ivan Allen said he did too. I slept well that night.

The next morning the September sun was out early, hot and bright on our back deck. Tall pines and maple trees offered ample shade, making the deck a perfect place to have breakfast. Before eating I opened the morning paper and saw my picture on the front page under the caption: "A Big Win for Mitchell." I was as happy at that moment as I can ever remember being. The scrambled eggs, toast, and hot coffee got cold while I sat staring off into space and savoring this moment of sweet victory.

The cheerful, noisy, early morning voices of the neighborhood children as they waited on the corner of our street for the school bus brought me suddenly back to earth. It hit me then that I was now partly responsible for their education and that of 115,000 other students in Atlanta. I vowed to do the very best job I could for *every* student, whether black or white.

4

Crisis in the Bible Belt

Although the primary election and runoff were held in September, the new Atlanta officeholders were not sworn in until January 3, 1962. As I prepared to assume my new responsibilities, I had a chance to take stock at midlife.

Ray and I were empty nesters now, but we stayed in our house on Club Drive, which was fairly large for the times. I wouldn't have minded moving to something smaller, but Ray did not want even to consider a new home. We rattled around in the big house, having less and less in common.

I never spoke to Ray about my views on civil rights, and he never shared any of his, but we knew instinctively that we were far apart on the issue. At about this time, I recall, we went to the beach for a vacation. During our drive, a prosperous-looking black man in a big, new Cadillac drove up alongside our Oldsmobile. I could see Ray's face muscles tighten and hear his voice become tense and disgusted as he said, "Look at that black man in that car. Who does he think he is?" Hearing these words, I knew once more that our once happy marriage was slowly but surely being eroded.

Indeed, like so many marriages that are not based on mutual admiration, respect, and honest communication, ours became more and more formally polite, silent, unfulfilling, and ritualistic. We went to church, visited relatives, had the grandkids in for visits, celebrated holidays, attended a dinner dance at the club or a work-related cocktail party—and that was all. I absorbed myself in my many activities and avoided thinking about the problems in my marriage.

For years, starting well before I entertained any political aspirations, my most time-consuming activities outside the home had involved school and church. I had always been active in the PTA at the schools attended by my children. By 1961, I had been teaching a Sunday school class for young married couples for nearly seven years, and I would continue to teach it until 1964. I loved the challenge, the dialogue, and above all the camaraderie, the parties, and the weekend mountain retreats. Ray preferred to stay home and play golf.

But the civil rights era raised fresh questions for me about the church. I couldn't understand how the terrible injustices we southern whites were inflicting on blacks could be justified, given the words of the Bible (Galatians 3:26,28): "For in Christ Jesus you are all sons of God through faith. . . . There is neither Jew or Greek, there is neither slave or free, there is neither male or female for you are one in Christ Jesus." How could segregation be right when "God is no respecter of persons" and "God shows no partiality"? The Bible seemed to mandate reconciliation: "behold how good and pleasant it is when brothers dwell in unity."

At the historical moment when the white churches of the Bible Belt most needed to prove their Christianity, they failed miserably. The shame of their stand against integration will endure as a blot on their history. Still, I was perhaps wrong to expect the southern church to take a stand on the side of racial justice. Most churches were, and still are, some of the most segregated organizations on earth.

I spent long years in the service of the Methodist church. I therefore feel qualified to comment on the conduct of the southern churches with some measure of expertise, especially where segregation is concerned. The burning issue of racial integration did not exist, did not even come up, until the late 1950s. Prior to that time the Peachtree Road Methodist Church set aside one Sunday a year to observe "Race Relations Sunday."

Observation of Race Relations Sunday was required by the national governing body of the Methodist church in a memorandum sent down from the office in New York City. When we observed the occasion, however, our ministers always played it safe. Their sermons were pure rhetoric, nothing more than a mild plea for better cooperation between the races. One minister did tell us about visiting Paine College in Augusta, Georgia, and asked the congregation for money to help support the school. From the looks of the college (which I later visited), our collections must have been small. Huge oak trees on the campus could not hide the construction shortcuts, lack of landscaping, and other problems that bespoke poverty.

The central governing body of the Methodist church was making an effort to effect change in its southern outposts. The problem was not the policy but the membership's reluctance to accept it. As early as 1952 a declaration of the Central Conference stated "that to discriminate against a person upon the basis of his race is both unfair and unchristian."

Despite all of the Bibles that are read, all the sermons preached, and all the Sunday school lessons taught, millions of church members are responsible for unchristian acts of discrimination, hatred, and even cruelty to blacks. At the same time many southerners, because of their religious backgrounds, have lived with high standards of right and wrong and have made personal sacrifice for their fellow man. My mother and grandmother were representative and set good examples for me.

In the 1860s and earlier, some southerners spoke out against the Civil War just as many more spoke out in favor of justice and freedom for blacks in the 1960s. For years I had kept a copy of Roy McLain's sermon entitled "Is Racial Integration the Answer?" which he delivered on June 24, 1956. *Time* had named McLain, the minister of the First Baptist Church of Atlanta, one of the ten best ministers in America. As a longtime admirer of his sermons I was shocked, surprised, and disappointed when I reread this one. In it he accused the National Association for the Advancement of Colored People (NAACP) of "tightening tensions and deepening the rivers of distrust." According to McLain, Jesus never "forced his affections on anyone. Forced integration is an assault on freedom of speech."

Now, less than a decade later, white churches began to experience a series of "pray-ins," occasions when blacks attended to find out whether churches were practicing as well as preaching God's Word. Pray-ins drew great cries of indignation from congregations. Blacks were widely accused of "coming not to worship but only to make trouble." The critics accused the black worshipers of being "insincere"—ironic indeed, in view of the patent insincerity among white churchgoers formulating the accusations.

At this time in my life I belonged to Saint James Methodist, which was nearer our home. The church's governing board produced a policy of sorts to deal with pray-ins: "If a Negro tries to enter our church he is to be met by two ushers at the door who will escort him/her to the back row. [We had no balcony.] The two ushers are to remain seated one on each side of the Negro." This policy statement was actually read in a solemn, sanctimonious voice, as if to establish once and for all that Saint James was showing its generous, Christian spirit. I was one of two women members of the thirty-person Board of Stewards when the vote was taken on this policy. Only three members out of thirty voted against it. This vote was the final blow for me. How could I continue to attend this church and be a "sincere" worshiper?

The pray-ins became front-page news and produced a rash of letters to the editor. One read: "The Negro students who flooded several white churches did not go to those churches to worship God. Their actions and statement at the churches displayed their hypocrisy and proved that they went to white churches to create trouble, seek publicity, and learn the reaction of whites. Their reasons were palpably ulterior." The editor of the *Atlanta Constitution,* much to my delight, appended the comment "Judge not that ye be not judged."

Another correspondent observed: "Isn't it enough that the taxpayer, the ones who must surrender their privacy, their parks and schools, and accept them [blacks] in every way, must now give up their pews in church also—the last decent place they can go to seek peace?" At the conclusion of his letter he declared, "I have no race hatred in my heart."

Rereading these letters I cannot help but recall the words of Martin Luther King, Jr.: "On sweltering summer days and crisp autumn mornings I have looked at the South's beautiful churches with their lofty spires pointing heavenly. Over and over, I have found myself asking, 'What kind of people worship here? Who is their God?'"

I did feel a measure of sympathy for ministers who ignored the race problem, because to take a stand meant losing your job. One liberal minister told me he kept quiet and stayed on at his church because, "blind though my members are, they still need the Word of God. They still need me to officiate at baptisms, christenings, marriages and funerals." Another told me, "If I should resign tomorrow, my congregation would call a Bible-quoting, fund-raising, Negro-hating preacher to take my place as quickly as possible." Many churches were paying off mortgages on their new, expensive church buildings. "If I left my church," another man of the cloth told me, "I would leave the members in a financial bind. I could not walk out on that responsibility."

Because of the uproar caused by the pray-ins, some eighty ministers in Atlanta came together long enough on November 3, 1957, to compose a "Ministers' Manifesto" that outlined their collective opinions on the segregation issue. I found nothing brave in the document. It read in part: "As Americans and Christians we have an obligation to obey the law. Hatred and scorn for those of another race, or for those who hold positions different from our own, cannot be maintained."

I read the entire manifesto carefully without finding in it any mention of love or justice. It made no mention of the centuries of suffering and offered no praise for the patience that blacks had exhibited. There was no reference to the brotherhood of man. I couldn't help wondering what Jesus would have thought if he had read the ministers' words.

I believe it was Mark Twain who once wrote: "If Jesus Christ came back to earth the one thing he would not be is a Christian." After seeing how the southern white churches greeted the civil rights movement, I would have to agree with him.

Unlike other white southern churches, the Unitarian Fellowship had no racial "seating policy." Anyone was welcome to attend. After I had been on the Board of Education for a year or two, Dr. Eugene Pickett, the Unitarian minister, called me one day to ask a favor: "We want permission to use the Tenth Street Elementary School on Sundays until our new building on North Druid Hills Road is completed."

I told him I would look into his request and call him back. I found that the Atlanta Board of Education had a written policy stating that "any organized church can hold services in a school so long as they have plans to build." Despite these words, even in the mid-1960s, after integration had begun, another policy, well known but unwritten, said that Atlanta's public schools could not be used as meeting places for blacks and whites together. I asked Dr. John Letson, the school superintendent, whether he would recommend that the school board grant the Unitarians' request without mentioning the presence of black members in the congregation. I was relieved and grateful when he agreed. The matter came up at the next board meeting, and I held my breath, but the request was granted without a dissenting vote. The other board members (one of whom was black) probably did not even know that any white church had black members.

Quakers and Unitarians also helped by supporting black students and their parents during the early months of school integration. I was invited to attend Sunday afternoon sessions given by the Unitarians to discuss the problems of the first black students. Dr. Robert Coles, a Harvard sociologist, moderated these meetings, which helped me understand and sympathize with the students' plight. I promptly took the problems that were identified to board meetings so that I could give my fellow members a more personal, albeit secondhand, understanding of the black students' perspective.

The Unitarians also asked white students and school faculties to be "fair, friendly and understanding. . . . please ask the newly transferred black students to eat with you in the cafeteria, walk with you in the halls, and include them as you would anyone in your school activities."

The Mennonites and the First Christian Church made contributions as well. They sent volunteers from their northern churches. Most helpful of all were the white teachers who agreed to teach in black schools. I doubt that any of us gave them appropriate credit and recognition at the time.

I found it ironic that white Protestant churches, which in some instances were literally next-door neighbors to schools, were sending exactly the opposite message with their restrictive seating policies. How could it be Christian to sit by a black in school yet refuse to sit by one at church? What a mixed message for the young minds of the students!

During the 1950s and 1960s the churches were being weakened not only by their unrelenting stand on segregation but also by affluence. Many of Atlanta's Northside churches had wealthy congregations. The fact came home to me when I visited the old Capitol Avenue School, situated in one of Atlanta's poorest white downtown neighborhoods. The principal showed me a closet full of old clothes and canned goods she had collected. I admired her for seeing after the physical needs of her pupils, but I wondered why some nearby church could not take on this charitable task and leave her school free to concentrate on educating the students.

I drove away from the visit disturbed and puzzled. On the next block I saw a large, handsome Methodist church and wondered why its members did not feed and clothe the obviously needy children. Then the answer came to me. This particular Methodist church, once affluent, was now bereft of its wealthy members. They had long since moved to the white suburbs, and the remaining few members were hard-pressed to pay the mortgage and the minister's salary as well. But what about the rich suburban churches to which the affluent members now belonged? Why didn't they help?

Since I belonged to one such wealthy church, I knew the answer. The wealthy churches were building million-dollar sanctuaries and large recreational centers, with buses to carry privileged children to sporting events where they could compete with other overprivileged children.

A close friend who is a member of Atlanta's First Presbyterian Church told me that one Sunday the congregation stood and sang a hymn with the words "Oh, what a worm am I." She said she looked around at the fashionably dressed women and the business tycoons and wondered whether any of them really felt like a worm.

One morning I picked up the phone to hear the lovely accent of an English friend. She said, "I'm in charge of the Summer Forum Series at Atlanta University. I want you to be one of the speakers." I was flattered, since Atlanta University was the graduate school of a complex of five black colleges. I felt apprehensive about speaking before such a large audience of black students, who might well ask themselves, "What's this white woman doing talking to us?" Still, I took the plunge and said yes.

When the morning of my talk came, I looked out over the audience of some 700 black students and decided to begin with a civil rights joke I had just heard.

A black Baptist preacher in New Jersey confided to his wife that he had been praying to the Lord for a "call" to preach in another part of the country and that finally the "call" had come. "From where?" she asked. "From Jackson, Mississippi," he replied. "JACKSON, MISSISSIPPI!!" she exclaimed. "Well, you just go back and pray to the Lord for more guidance." After some time the preacher came out. "What did the Lord say?" his wife wanted to know. "The Lord said he'd go with me as far as Memphis, Tennessee."

Fortunately the joke brought much laughter. I told the audience that I had picked my own topic. "I'm going to speak on the civil rights movement from the white perspective. I have chosen the title 'Confronted/Compelled.'"

I seldom write out a speech. Instead I make an outline that will help me stay on track. I still have the notes for this one. I began by speaking of the need for action.

—When your house—the South—is on fire, you don't go out and work in your rose garden. . . .

Who is my brother? Everyone is my brother/sister and all that implies. I care about him. I share with him. I suffer when he suffers. I take pride in his accomplishments. I want him to have the same advantages and pleasures I have. . . .

I do not believe that God ordained one race to be superior to another. I do not believe He favors any race. . . . I believe in the brotherhood of all mankind. . . .

I believe that the southern white churches have sinned so greatly in their treatment of blacks that they would not recognize the truth now if it came marching down the street. The churches' discriminatory policies have been, and are, unchristian in the extreme. . . .

Our minds are twisted to shape the truth as men proclaimed it, not as the prophets of old knew and proclaimed it from the mountaintop. . . .

I closed with a quotation from the prophet Amos. "Let justice roll down like waters, and righteousness like an ever-flowing stream."

In the 1960s my talks were usually given before smaller audiences and were seldom covered by the press. I always said whatever I felt like saying. This time, much to my surprise, reporters from the *Atlanta Constitution* and the *Atlanta Journal* were present. When I had finished, two reporters came up on the stage and asked me, "Did you really mean what you said? Did you say that the churches in the South had sinned so much on the race issue that they wouldn't know the truth if they heard it?" I affirmed my statement. I knew firsthand how miserably most southern white churches had failed to dispense brotherly love or justice to blacks.

On the way home I stopped in town to have lunch with a good friend, who asked how the speech had gone. As usual before going home I also stopped to get groceries and tend to a few errands. When I walked in the house, the phone was ringing. It was my friend. She said, "I thought you told me your speech went okay."

"Well," I said, "that was my impression."

"Go get your evening paper," she urged. "You're quoted on the front page, two columns wide with your picture. You're going to have some upset, angry church members—to say nothing of an upset, angry husband."

I went back outside and picked up the paper from the driveway. Sure enough, there I was, under the headline, "Racial Solution Held Church Job."

Mrs. Ray (Sara) Mitchell, member of the Atlanta Board of Education, Tuesday laid the responsibility for solving the moral issue of racial segregation at the feet of the churches.

In a speech to an integrated audience of 700 at Clark College she said, "Now that the legal question is almost completely settled, the church must solve the moral question." "Guilt and untruth have been preached all over the South," she said.

Mrs. Mitchell accused Southern churches of offering no leadership at a time when people most need it. "They have practiced so many sins they can't preach the truth," she said.

"This is not a blanket indictment against all churches and ministers," Mrs. Mitchell pointed out. "But if the church does not meet this challenge," she predicted, "it is going to sound its own death knell."

"Churches must declare a policy on the issue," she said. "Segregated seating in the church is no policy." Mrs. Mitchell urged all to "confront this burning question of the day and not avoid it."

She told the predominately Negro audience, white people are "searching our souls" for an answer. "Even the ranters and ravers are trying to come to peace" with themselves, she said.

"This question tears families apart, separates friends, pits whites against one another. You cannot hate," the 8th Ward school board member told the group. "Integrationists have to get along with segregationists."

The board member said she will continue to speak out on important issues even at the expense of possibly losing her place on the board.

"I would rather say what I want to say in four years," she said, "than stay eight or 12 years and say nothing."

I asked myself what Ray would say. I knew I couldn't simply hide the paper and say, "I guess they missed our house tonight." Ray read the paper every day, so he'd just drive to the drugstore for another one. I braced for the worst and went about preparing dinner as if nothing extraordinary had happened.

When Ray saw the article, he made no attempt to hide his anger. He was appalled—visibly shaken—to read on the front page that his wife had denounced the church in such strong language. More than 100,000 people, including his friends and bosses at Retail Credit Company, would see every scandalous word. His anger was the more intense because he vigorously disagreed with my liberal viewpoint, although people who didn't know better might reasonably have assumed that, as husband and wife, we saw eye to eye. Ray's name was even the first thing in the article!

That evening I received the first of many, many phone calls. It came from a woman irate to the point of sounding hysterical. Unfortunately Ray answered the phone.

From fifteen feet away I could hear the voice screaming, "Your wife should be impeached!" She meant "recalled," and Ray agreed with her—or at least I got that impression from his response. He seemed to believe that this woman represented collective opinion as measured by a Gallup poll. I found Ray's reaction upsetting but not the words of my caller. I was used to such responses by then.

The next morning's edition of the *Atlanta Constitution* carried the same story with a big spread and a lead editorial. Then the calls began in earnest, and the letters. The people who disagreed with my liberal stand virtually all made telephone calls. People with the mentality of Ku Klux Klan members, I found, don't write letters. There were two exceptions. One correspondent wrote: "Dearest Huney Child, You sound as though you are a sister of Ralph McGill's or Gene Patterson's [editor of the *Constitution*]. Same ole hawg wash from the do-good-ers in Atlanta." The letter seemed to me a lefthanded compliment. Someone else wrote, "You have arrived. You have become notorious like 'Rastus' McGill, and 'Luther' King, Jr. One who suffers with consti-pation of thought and diarrhea of words, when they disgorge them-selves of mental garbage and venom, surely must feel relieved. Hope you are feeling well today."

Of course neither of these two writers signed his name. People who agreed with me, on the other hand, wrote letters not only to me but also to editors. All of these correspondents signed their names.

"I think many sincere Christians want to hear these voices cry-ing in the wilderness of deep rooted prejudices for they know they are wrong."

"I am writing to let you know I am with you 100 percent in your outspoken convictions, and have great admiration for your courage. The New South needs people like you and Ralph McGill badly if it is to ever progress in our new modern space age world."

"To be frank I can't remember whether I voted for you or not, but I will next time."

"I agree that most of our churches have remained silent when they should have spoken out."

"I too am a Methodist and appreciate your courage in speaking out."

These last letters were not only personally encouraging but also, I felt, tapped a reservoir of goodwill toward blacks that many segregationists did not know existed.

Doris Lockerman, a columnist for the *Atlanta Constitution,* accurately predicted what would occur after my public denouncement of the southern church: "Sara, your dissenters will rise up to curse you. Your telephone will ring off the hook, and when you answer you will hear only a click, or worse, an epithet. Your name will be taken off invitation lists. The patronizing smiles you have had because you are a woman will harden into glares or cease entirely."

At first my harassment by the Ku Klux Klan, after all this publicity, was hard to prove. In fact, it was several days before I began to suspect anything. Sometimes when I answered the phone I would hear only heavy breathing followed by a click. Next came callers who would say in a loud, rough, uncouth voice something like, "You want your children to marry niggers? You want your grandchildren to be black? Ha, ha, ha." No Klan member called with a clear message. No one ever told me why he disagreed with what I said about the church. The messages always consisted of senseless rambling and obscenities.

As the days passed, the calls became more numerous and uglier. I figured the Atlanta Klan had given my phone number to all their members with special instructions to call late at night or early in the morning between 4:00 and 6:00 A.M. Naturally this timing upset Ray. Even though at this point in our very strained marriage we slept in separate bedrooms, he could hear the phone ring. After about three nights of nuisance calls, I put the receiver between the mattress and box springs of my bed. Then all I could hear was a faint buzz, nothing loud enough to keep me awake.

A friend asked why I didn't get an unlisted number. "What," I said, "and miss all those weird, fascinating people? Who else do I know who has had such an experience?" I regretted not being a psychologist. I learned that some minds work in strange, revealing ways. Callers would start talking to anyone who answered. To my younger son, Perry, when he was home from Duke University, the caller would say something like, "How do you like having a mother who is a nigger lover?" He would answer, "I like having a mother who can love all people, no matter what the color of their skin. We'll see you in church Sunday, okay?" Fortunately, Ray seldom answered the phone. During this period, Perry, who was on my side, and I made sure that one of us reached it first.

Not all the calls were obscene. Most often the caller would begin by saying I was a disgrace to the white race, to my southern ancestors, to the church. I never replied, and toward the end of their tirades the callers would always wind down. Then if they mentioned anything I could make a reasonable comment on, I did.

One woman finished her hate-filled spiel and happened to mention that she lived in the Grant Park section of Atlanta. By this time I had begun to make a game of seeing if I could somehow turn my callers around, calm them down, so I told her I had attended a campaign rally there when I was running for office. "It was put on by a labor union," I said, "and someone brought the most delicious carrot cake I ever ate." There was a long pause on the end of the line. Then I heard her say, "Honey, do you want the recipe?"

One night about midnight a man called who was not in the mood to be turned around. I heard his rude, husky voice say, "You had better not go near your front door. If you do you won't live long enough to get back into your house." He breathed heavily into the phone for a few more seconds. When I said nothing he hung up.

I had a hard time believing that anyone would really try to kill me. I wasn't important enough in the civil rights arena. Even so, I decided to call police headquarters and report the threat to my life. A female operator answered my call. She sounded unimpressed to the point of boredom as she offered to connect me with Homicide.

Another voice, male this time, answered. "What's that again?" I repeated, "My life has been threatened." "I'll connect you to another line," he said, even more unconcerned.

I finally reached someone paid to listen to crazy people who thought their life was in danger. "Where do you live?" he asked. I told him I was on Club Drive, about nine miles from downtown.

"Don't worry," he assured me. "Klan members won't come out to your neighborhood. They don't even know where it is. Now, if you lived on the South side of town, the situation might call for some action." I was white, in other words, and I lived on the "right" side of town. There was no way I could compare my situation with that confronting black civil rights workers.

I got in bed and went to sleep, thankful for my good fortune—and even more admiring of all the people who were indeed putting their lives on the line for the sake of justice and brotherhood.

Why did my publicized criticism of the church so rile the Klan? As nearly as I could determine, its members actually believed they had a very close tie with God and therefore with His church. According to them, God had ordained the separation of the races. I had said I believed that God wanted all men to be brothers. One of us had to be wrong, and in their eyes it wasn't the Klan.

I was a sinner in the Klansmen's sight. I was also a "godless, Communist degenerate," one who had to be chastised. But being a native, white, southern "lady" saved me from a worse fate than obscene calls in the night and a threat on my life. The midnight and early morning calls continued for four months before ending abruptly on November 22, 1963, the day President John Kennedy was assassinated.

Because I couldn't reconcile my core beliefs about what Christianity was meant to be with the church's lack of racial leadership (and in fact its tacit approval of segregation), in 1964 I finally gave up the adult Sunday school class I had taught for more than fifteen years. I just couldn't continue, especially as I began wanting more and more to address the failure of white Christians to embrace integration.

In one lesson, I wanted to examine the frequent excuse that the North was as guilty of race prejudice as the South. "While this may be true," I told my class, "we must forget about the sins of other sections of America. We in the South have been and still are guilty of such base, cruel, dishonest, indifferent, pious, self-righteous actions against blacks that it staggers the imagination."

I found the perfect Scripture, too, in Matthew 7:3,5: "Why behold thou the mote that is in thy brother's eye, but consider not the beam that is in thy own eye? Thou hypocrite, first cast out the beam from thy own eye; and then shalt thou see clearly to cast out the mote from thy brother's eye."

Dr. Nat Long, our minister, who had gone with me to Atlanta's first integrated political rally in 1947, approved of my lessons, and so did the doctrine of the Methodist Church U.S.A., but our local membership was not changing. I was clearly out of step with local beliefs. My convictions and my theological readings were pulling me away from my family's beliefs and especially from the particularly strict religious beliefs of my husband. But I had long known better than to discuss my lessons with Ray.

When I stopped going to church, I heard that some members missed me. People asked, "Whatever happened to that nice Mrs. Mitchell who used to help with the church night suppers, keep the children during church service, and teach a class of adults?" I also heard the answer, "She got involved in the civil rights movement and doesn't have time for the Lord's work anymore."

But I felt that the Lord's work was exactly what I was doing. After all, I was working for better race relations and better educational advantages for black students. What was the Lord's work I was abandoning? Cooking church suppers for overfed members, filling my pew on Sunday morning to hear sermons that began with little jokes and continued with sophistry, contributing money that helped pay for green velvet pew cushions? I actually felt that I had been "born again" but in a new and different light. I was beginning to see a much better way to use my time and money.

I agreed with Samuel Miller of Harvard Divinity School, who said, "Only one kind of religion counts today and that is the kind which is radical enough to engage in this world's basic troubles." I also concurred with John Lewis, a civil rights Freedom Rider and now a congressman from Atlanta, who said, "I saw more God in the movement than in the church."

On the other hand, I recall the words of the late Hubert H. Humphrey: "In a broad sense, religious elements have been the most important force at work today in behalf of civil rights." I agreed with him up to a point, but until the late 1960s (at the earliest) in the South, this "most important force" was coming 90 percent from black churches and barely 10 percent from white churches.

Many of the black churches in Atlanta set aside one day a year as "Woman's Day." After I came to know many of the city's black schoolteachers by virtue of my position on the school board, I was often asked to speak on Woman's Day. At first I had misgivings, because even though I had taught a large adult Sunday school class for many years, I had never been asked to fill the pulpit at the big eleven o'clock service, but I decided to try to rise to the challenge, qualified or not.

My first "sermon" was entitled "Divine Discontent." In it I said that we Christians should work to improve our world *now,* during our lifetimes and those of our children, without waiting for some other better world (or heaven) to come or for someone else to take on the job. I added, "The fact that you've invited a white woman to fill your pulpit is proof enough of your forgiving love towards my race."

I am sorry to report that many of the black churches I later visited as a speaker on Woman's Day were making the same mistake as the white churches that I have criticized and were setting the same poor example for their members. Some black churches, for example, placed the same importance on outward appearances. Their church buildings were often larger and more expensive than they could afford. Out in front, in a prominent parking space labeled "pastor," there was frequently a big, ostentatious car.

And I couldn't help noticing how many offerings were being taken in those churches on Sunday mornings—three at a minimum. One was often even taken for the guest speaker, much to my embarrassment. I always contributed the money right back to Woman's Day, without ever knowing how much it was.

When I sat in front of these congregations in the early 1960s and gazed into the eyes of the overworked and underpaid maids and janitors, I wanted to shout, "God has all He needs! He wants you to keep your money to feed and get better health care for yourself and your family. God loves *you,* not this expensive sanctuary and your minister's fine car."

Many of my observations on the black church and their ministers were seconded by at least one outspoken black minister, the Reverend Isaac Richmond. His guest editorial in the *Atlanta Voice* during the period read:

> If, as a people, we have supported do-nothing religious leaders for a century of further enslavement, it appears only logical that we must now begin to support, with our money, black men who are truly sacrificing for the struggle for black liberation.
>
> In the past the black church has been concerned about what kind of meat people eat rather than whether people had meat to eat. Church dogma has been built around proving and disproving the legitimacy of this or that denomination, instead of relating to the salvation of a world bent on destroying itself. Black preachers are more concerned about who sleeps together than they are about who has a place to sleep.

From one end of the world to the other on Sunday morning we hear of the sins of mankind by some kind of preacher. But I ask you, who is the biggest pimp in the black community? Who drives the biggest Cadillac? Who takes trips to the Holy Land by taxing the poor? Who comes back with "Holy dirt, holy water and holy prayer cloths" to sell to the faithful believers for the salvation of his soul? Who gets a salary for bleeding the poor?

Everybody in the black community knows. But, nobody will do anything about it. It is time that the black community take a long look and a serious look at black religion.

In a follow-up editorial, Reverend Richmond wrote:

How many Sunday school teachers actually tell black children concretely that the Christian religion was designed to make black people docile and consenting slaves? The "Jesus will do it syndrome" is the first psychological pitfall in the struggle for black liberation. If Jesus is in fact going to do it all, the answer to what I am supposed to do is NOTHING, and that is precisely what most black people are doing about their oppression.

The church has become a therapeutic sanctuary for those who want to talk but are not committed enough to act.

I don't know what being "saved" is but I know what being lost is. Lost is slavery, economic exploitation, political impotency, police brutality, slumlords, hunger, poverty, miseducation, black leaders being shot, jailed and hounded by racist police, and a group of lying preachers who perceive their jobs as one of keeping black masses insensitive to their condition.

All in all, during the early 1960s, my religious beliefs and my now-active civil rights conscience collided. In the ensuing battle, traditional white southern Methodist ideology lost. I also lost a few more conservative friends. My husband and I grew even further apart.

I recall that during this time I had struck up an acquaintance with a nice black preacher whom I had met at several rallies. It turned out that he sometimes did work around people's homes, so I hired him to come over and wax our living room and dining room floors. As he was finishing the job, Ray came in from playing golf and asked how much the man wanted. When the preacher said, "Well, I think $8.50 would be right," Ray hit the ceiling. He couldn't understand how three hours of hard, sweaty work by a black man could be worth $8.50. In Ray's eyes it was robbery! I was terribly embarrassed. I don't even remember what Ray finally agreed to pay, but I do know that my heart sank, and it hardened against Ray, too.

My heart and mind were clearly not at home or at church but at political meetings and at stimulating lunches and in phone conversations I had with liberal friends of both races. In other words, I was eager to put my liberal beliefs to work at last. My heart and mind were working together on the job I had campaigned so hard to win. It was now up to me to work on behalf of *all* of Atlanta's students.

5

"Men Don't Like Women on Boards"

My first four-year term on the Atlanta Board of Education began January 3, 1962. It was the first and only job "outside the home," as they say, that I held during my thirty years of marriage, and it was considered a part-time position. This was a sort of elected citizens' advisory board whose role was to oversee what our public school administrators were doing to improve the education of our youth and how they were spending Atlantans' tax dollars. The top administrators answered to the superintendent, and he or she was hired by the board.

As I've mentioned before, my salary was just $200 a month. Board members were legally required only to attend our one official meeting each month. No member took the job for the money. Half the members had much bigger fish to fry, and the rest of us regarded our salaries as little more than honorariums.

I was the exception. To me, the salary meant that I was more than Mrs. Ray Mitchell, more than the good, quiet corporate wife, more than a mother of three and the manager of a household (albeit one now virtually empty, both physically and emotionally), more than a volunteer with opinions people could take or leave. After my election, I felt validated in many ways. The official check for $200 proved that Atlantans thought I was worthy of representing them.

The agenda for our monthly meetings was set by the superintendent. We members received a copy five days in advance, sometimes along with background material on the subjects to be covered. We also attended a so-called briefing session the night before the monthly meeting. The superintendent ostensibly wanted board members to be fully informed of the agenda items. What Letson really wanted was to know how we would vote, so that he wouldn't be surprised or embarrassed. The briefing was described as "open," but dinner was served first. Reporters and members of the public were reluctant to sit and watch us eat and were thereby discouraged from attending.

Parents and teachers called us with their concerns. We were also permitted to research and propose topics that we believed merited the board's attention. One of my main campaign promises had been to work full time for the students of Atlanta, since my children were all grown. So I found plenty to do to earn that $200, starting with the basics.

At first the board met in a small building that was located in the back of City Hall, but then an auditorium was found across the street. We needed this larger space, because our audiences had nearly tripled with the controversy over integration. Sometimes well over 250 people were present. When there was a large crowd, people were usually very mad about something.

There was a raised dais and fancy, high-backed black leather chairs, which I found rather pretentious. Letson sat dead center and presided over our meeting. I was assigned the far seat on one side, and the female secretary of the board sat in the other. I never knew the rationale behind the seat assignments.

There were nine members (an uneven number to avoid tie votes)—seven white males, one black male, and me. Although I was replacing a female incumbent, the men evidently decided to act like jolly good fellows. They emphasized that they were glad to have me aboard, glad that I was now "a member of the team." I wasn't totally sure what game the team was playing, but my experience as an observer for the League of Women Voters made me apprehensive.

For my part, I had made enough bold statements during the campaign to cause the men to feel some apprehension, too. Virtually all rookie candidates speak of "the changes I will make when I am elected." Although I had tried to keep such bravado to a minimum, I'm sure I was somewhat guilty of it. My fellow board members had heard me night after night at the campaign rallies. They knew where I stood on the issues facing Atlanta's schools, especially integration.

But I quickly learned that before I could fulfill even one promise requiring a vote, a majority of the members had to vote with me. I was innocent of the first important rule of officeholding: make friends with members whose vote you need. During the campaign I had promised, "In the approaching transition period of the Atlanta schools (desegregation) I will work in harmony with the school superintendent, the board, and the administration." I did make an effort, but how could I play on a team that had been, and still was, condoning segregation?

Board members had spent the last several years in countless secret meetings. They had squandered on lawyers thousands of dollars that should have gone to educate students—all with the intent of slowing integration to a crawl. I wasn't playing in the same ball park, let alone on the same team.

Four of the nine board members were bankers. Atlanta schools had an annual budget that was over $60 million and was increasing each year. This pool of funds circulated among the city's four major banks, spending one year with each, and so each bank encouraged one of its executives to run for the board to ensure that all would go smoothly when its turn came. A suitable candidate who could be elected was more or less "chosen," and the necessary campaign funds were forthcoming. The bankers were nice enough fellows, but I often wondered how dedicated they were to the education of students, especially black students, even on a separate-but-equal basis.

One incident illustrates the typical performance of the banking clique on the board. The Citizen's Trust Bank of Atlanta was the South's largest black-owned bank. I was urged by the black business establishment to ask the board to include this bank in their four-year cycle of white banks, which would allow each bank a turn every five years instead of every four. From the response, I gathered that a more revolutionary suggestion had never been made in the board's history. "Citizen's Trust is not equipped to handle the business," I was told. Many other specious arguments were put forth, but the seed had been planted. Four years later, after determined opposition and stalling, Citizen's Trust was finally included in the cycle.

As I have said, the board had a black male member. He was Dr. Rufus Clement, president of Atlanta University. In him I should have had a strong ally, or he should have had a strong ally in me. After all, he was the first black ever to be elected to the board. When I arrived, Dr. Clement had already served a term.

In fact, Dr. Clement was one of the very first blacks since Reconstruction to win a citywide race. Some people said he won because his title was impressive and because voters didn't know he was black. His picture never appeared in a campaign ad or on television. I was impressed by his obvious intelligence and his long years of experience in the field of education.

As a liberal newcomer, I had counted heavily on Dr. Clement's friendship and support. But all too soon I began to realize that we weren't in sync. At one meeting, for example, I moved that we investigate the constant complaint that black schools were getting used books left over from white schools. The school superintendent dismissed the allegation, saying, "Oh, that's just one of those rumors you hear from a few disgruntled parents." I knew better, having heard many black parents and teachers say, "The only textbooks available to us are hand-me-downs, stamped with the name of a white school, complete with a white child's signature." Dr. Clement did not even second my motion to begin discussion on the issue.

On another occasion when the board was discussing an issue that affected a black school, I felt I understood what the problem was, and I said so. Dr. Clement cut me off. "Mrs. Mitchell, how could you understand? You aren't black." But in the opinion of many people in the black community, Dr. Clement did not think like a black himself. An editorial in the black-owned *Atlanta Voice* in July 1962 carried the headline "Yet, There's a Negro on the School Board":

> Countless complaints have been made about the insufficient, inferior and segregated education to which Negro students in Atlanta have been subjected. Many of these complaints have been taken to the Atlanta School Board, only to be pushed back "for further study". . . . Yet, there is a Negro on the Board. . . .
>
> Some Negro students, after getting to school, must walk as far as three blocks to outdoor mobile units while changing classes, even when the temperature is below freezing. One Negro elementary school is even without a cafeteria. Yet, there is a Negro on the Board. . . .
>
> Though these deplorable conditions prevail, there is one member of the School Board who is showing an active concern to the extent of researching the matter and trying to initiate the badly needed changes.
>
> That Board member is Mrs. Sara Mitchell from the Eighth Ward, not a predominately Negro Ward. YET, THERE'S A NEGRO ON THE BOARD.

After talking to black friends and activists, and reading other reactions like the above, I came to realize that despite Dr. Clement's skin color and impressive background in education administration, he was not standing up for the causes I expected him to. But maybe the reason had to do with me as well. Maybe I rubbed him the wrong way. So after too many votes of eight against one in clearly racial matters, I decided to see whether there was a misunderstanding between us and, if so, to correct it.

I called Dr. Clement at Atlanta University and asked for an appointment. When I arrived in his large, handsome office I was kept waiting, although I saw no one around except his receptionist. I told Dr. Clement of my disappointment that our relationship was strained. "For some reason we aren't communicating, not understanding each other." I assured him I was only attempting to represent his race as well as I could. He listened with politeness and patience and forbearance. I finished by asking him whether I had offended him in any way.

Dr. Clement hesitated for a moment before speaking. "Mrs. Mitchell, men do not like women who make decisions."

I was stunned and hurt but managed to collect myself enough to say, "Dr. Clement, I have never made a decision since I came on the board. There are eight other members. Any decision has to be voted on by a majority." What I really wanted to say was: "I can no more help being a woman than you can help being black."

Dr. Clement, I began to understand, did not like women on boards or in public office of any kind. He believed that women belonged in the kitchen, bedroom, or nursery. Why had I assumed that a black man couldn't be just as big a male chauvinist as a white man? My visit scarcely solved the problem. If anything, the lines between us were more firmly drawn.

Yet I heard from Dr. Clement's family and friends that he was a good man. One night I sat next to him at a small dinner party. In that setting I found him to be a stimulating conversationalist, charming both to his wife and to me.

Dr. Clement died in about 1965 without our having attained even a cordial professional relationship as we worked to better the education of black children. I attended his funeral and walked down the long aisle of Sister's Chapel on the Spelman College campus, forming an honor guard with the other board members. I recall being impressed by the elaborate ceremony, the long and laudatory eulogies, and the chapel overflowing with mourners.

On the day of the funeral, as it happened, I had earlier been called about a meeting to be held after the service. The black "power structure" was convening to agree on a replacement for Dr. Clement's seat on the board. I was glad to sit in, although I wasn't optimistic about the outcome. My conservative fellow board members weren't about to appoint anyone with real integrationist leanings.

During the meeting, which was held in the conference room of a bank on Hunter Street, we suddenly heard a marching band. With one accord, we rose to our feet—ten black men and I—and rushed to the large front window. A football parade was coming down the street! I had never seen a football parade in the black section of town. What could be more fun on a glorious, warm fall day?

After the parade, feeling refreshed, we returned to our backroom politics and resumed our deliberations. At the next board meeting, someone I would call a typical white business type was appointed to fill the remaining months of Dr. Clement's term.

During my first days on the board, all eight men voted against me nearly 100 percent of the time. I was still able to play a valuable role in the black community by being a friend on the board. Many people called and came to see me about the shortcomings in their schools. I not only listened but called them about forthcoming agenda items that I knew these citizens were especially interested in. I mailed them background information. Often, before meetings started, I went into the audience and handed out material pertaining to the night's agenda items. I could and did see to it that members of the public at least aired their grievances before us.

For these simple acts of kindness I was rewarded with many generous compliments from the black community. I remember being especially pleased when one young black civil rights activist told me before a board meeting, "Just seeing you sitting there makes us feel good."

There is a scene in Spike Lee's movie *Malcolm X* that has made me question some of my memories about my work in the movement. In this scene, a young white woman approaches Malcolm X at Harvard after he has given a speech. She asks him, "What can a decent white person do to help your movement?" "Nothing," he answers abruptly and walks away. Can it be that I, and other women like me, offered nothing to the civil rights movement?

Although Atlanta's white, liberal-on-race women have never received credit, I believe that we made a real contribution. While we may not have been heroes on the front line, we offered heavy backup support for those who were. We helped black civil right workers bring about integration of schools and public accommodations, often at considerable personal cost.

I have no proof—no facts and no figures to document my statement. All I know is that we were treated as friends and coworkers by the black civil rights activists and leaders. They were kind and helpful. They welcomed us. We often sat around after a meeting, laughing and sharing stories. I never heard them express any criticism or any resentment of us.

The liberal women had the same cause as the blacks. We were determined that Atlanta would not become a Birmingham, a Little Rock, or a Selma, Alabama, with a George Wallace, a Bull Connor, water hoses, attack dogs, and cattle prods. So every morning during the late 1950s and 1960s we went out in the belief that we could help save the integrity of the city of Atlanta and even that of the state of Georgia.

We spent most of our days at interracial meetings plotting and planning our strategy to keep our schools open in the face of strong determination on the part of Governor Ernest Vandiver and the state legislature that not one black child would ever attend school with a white child. Our best ally was the press—the reporters who covered our meetings, published our letters to the editor, and joined us in our efforts to keep our schools open and public. Members of the press, along with a few astute businessmen, could see that closing the schools would spell economic catastrophe.

After too long a delay, the Supreme Court interceded, and our schools were integrated. Then liberal women became busier than ever. We began meeting with the first integrated black students and their parents to hear their many legitimate complaints. We talked to school administrators and teachers. We accompanied black parents to their first PTA meetings and introduced them to the teachers and staffs and other parents.

When the public accommodation law was passed in 1964 and Atlanta's restaurants were integrated, we invited our black friends to have lunch and dinner with us. If a beauty salon employed a black hair stylist, we made an appointment with her. When the public parks opened their pools to blacks (and were nearly deserted) we took our families there to swim. We invited blacks to our homes and to parties, and we introduced them to our like-minded friends. We welcomed them into our homes and our lives.

I know that these efforts on our part were very small compared with the bigger battles fought for civil rights. Still, these were things that we white women could do. We did them to the best of our ability, willingly and gladly.

Who were these "liberal" women from the north side of town? Many had come to Atlanta with their husbands from up north. Many were Jewish. A few were native southerners. Most were well off financially, and most were college graduates.

While women like me were involved in the everyday life of the city, going to meetings, speaking to PTAs, church groups, and enjoying a pleasant social life, many others were working for civil rights at a cost in sacrifice and suffering that I could hardly imagine. Nan Pendergrast, a civil rights friend, gave me a copy of a letter she received from a white "freedom worker," one who had gone to jail for her convictions. The young college student from Connecticut, writing from Fulton

County Jail, expressed her feelings of isolation and humiliation of being in jail. But she also expressed her belief that she thought she understood even more how blacks in the country felt. She also said that she believed she should be able to associate with whom she wanted and to protest when she thought something was wrong without being arrested. She ended the letter by stating that she had been made stronger by her arrest.

Many such letters and articles from white people like this young woman attest to the sacrifices they made for the civil rights movement.

In contrast, the civil rights action in which my white friends and I took part was not fraught with danger and death. We were fighting segregation in the schools, in white churches, in public eating places and restrooms. Our adversaries did not carry billy clubs, water hoses, whips, or handcuffs or have police dogs or carry guns. Instead we were laughed at, criticized, ostracized, ignored, booed, and shunned by segregationists and by many onetime friends. It seems to me that we paid a very small price in comparison to the hardships and sufferings of others—a very small price indeed.

Since many women actually do try harder in a political world that is still dominated by men, I set an ambitious goal for my first year in office: I would visit each school in Atlanta's entire system. In the 1960s we had 126 elementary schools and 28 high schools. My plan was to visit 4 schools a day, going three days a week. While I may have been the only board member to accomplish this feat, I was also the only one who didn't have a full-time job.

I began my visiting adventure fairly ignorant, not knowing exactly what I hoped to learn from the experience. I just felt that this was the way to embark on my career. I knew I wanted to meet as many principals, staff, and faculty as I could, and I wanted to see what condition our buildings and grounds were in. If possible, I wanted to get a feel for the amount of "learning" that was going on in each school. And given the glacial pace of Atlanta's just begun, one-grade-at-a-time integration plan, I wanted—despite the long-touted political rhetoric of "separate but equal" schools—to see for myself how well the doctrine worked.

I went unannounced, and most of the principals I met were polite, open, and friendly. Some were suspicious and guarded and took a minimum amount of time to show me around. Regardless of my reception, I carefully assessed the buildings and grounds. When I returned home I wrote my findings and opinions of each school on a 3 × 5 card that I could use at board meetings and when I responded to the concerns of parents and teachers.

Of Butler Elementary on Younge Street (around the corner from Ebenezer Baptist), I wrote: "Building 51 years old, almost no playground. Overcrowded and on double sessions for 19 years. *Note:* How can a child taught one half day for seven years compete with those taught for a full school day? Bring up at next board meeting."

About Ed S. Cook Elementary: "White school in deprived, low income area. Building old and worn out, grounds small. Principal told me, 'IQ average here 87th percentile.' Hard to believe when I looked in on the second grade class. Brightest kids I have seen anywhere."

About Thomasville Elementary: "Building cheaply constructed. Like many schools in black neighborhoods they may look good outside, but the inside shows clearly its shoddy construction. I felt sorry for the scared-of-a-board-member principal. I am just trying to be helpful but she probably thinks I am snooping. I couldn't tell much about this school so I walked around the building and grounds and left."

About Whiteford Elementary: "Has just been converted from a formerly all white school to a black one. Had 300 white students, now has 900 black ones. On double sessions, already needs relief. Bring this up at next meeting."

About Turner High (black): "Poorly built, ugly . . . narrow halls, no office space, no showers for athletic teams, 800 lockers for 1,600 students."

So it went. Before 1962 was over I had visited all 154 schools. When I began, all I could judge fairly were the buildings and grounds. By the time I had visited 50 schools, I could enter and immediately feel what kind of school it was, how much education was taking place, whether there was rapport between teachers and pupils, and whether the school was well run.

Our supposedly "separate but equal" black schools were operating under a number of terrible handicaps: too many students for the facility; too short a day, with many classes on double session; students using secondhand books (usually very outdated) from white schools; run-down buildings and grounds. In the 1960s large numbers of black pupils came from homes where parents were uneducated and where there was extreme poverty and malnutrition. Many lacked medical attention.

Otis Cochran, a twenty-one-year-old black civil rights activist, told me a revealing story:

> I attended Ware Elementary. One day I was sick, so my mother wrote an excuse for me. When I gave it to the teacher she looked surprised—"amazed" is a better word. Most of the parents at Ware had a hard time writing, much less finding the necessary pen and paper, or time, to write notes. My teacher showed my excuse around to the other teachers and then to the principal.
>
> My mother's well-expressed, well-written note meant all the difference in my education. From that day on, my teachers, realizing I was from a home where my parents were educated, gave me an extra measure of attention, helping me with my lessons anytime I needed it. . . . they didn't want me to get lost in the system.

The extra attention paid off. Some years later I saw Otis's picture in *Time*. He had won a scholarship to Yale University's law school.

During 1962–1963, desegregation was of course the hottest issue confronting Atlanta in general and our school board in particular. When these two forces collided head on, the impact could be explosive. The enforcement of fair housing laws, for example, finally meant to blacks that the federal government backed their desire to live in better neighborhoods. Unfortunately, whites unwilling to live next door to blacks fled the neighborhoods, with a predictable effect on the local schools.

Key Elementary School was one such early case. Originally built for 1,000 white students, in the fall of 1963 it found itself with fewer than 300. Furthermore, the three black schools nearby were all on double sessions. It was obvious to me that the board should turn Key into a school for blacks by assigning to it some of the nearby students on double sessions.

When word spread through the neighborhood surrounding the school that the board was considering turning Key School over to black pupils, the remaining whites were furious. I can still vividly recall arriving for the board's regular monthly meeting and finding our building besieged by an angry mob of at least 300 parents, relatives, and residents. I had to work my way up to the front door. There I encountered one of the school system's guards, who shouted, "Lady, nobody—and I mean *nobody*—else is coming in here. . . . it's already jam-packed!" He let me pass, embarrassed, when I told him I was a board member.

Our meeting room was indeed packed with muttering whites. On seeing such a large, angry crowd both outside and inside our building, Dr. Letson made a quick decision: the meeting would be moved over to the much larger City Hall chambers. Once the move had been accomplished, Dr. Letson again called the meeting to order. We had already agreed to put the Key School issue first on the agenda. But facing such outraged parents, for a few uneasy moments none of us seemed willing to make the appropriate motion. Finally, swallowing hard, I spoke up as forcefully as I could. "I move that to ease severe over-crowding in nearby schools, the board assign black students to Key Elementary."

So much shouting, screaming, and fist waving immediately erupted that we had to adjourn the meeting right then and there, before a vote had been taken. The guards had to call police, who arrived within five minutes and cleared the room. The audience (really a mob) then lay in wait for us in the City Hall's large lobby area, so the police had to clear people out of there as well. The crowd, knowing we had to leave sometime, then milled around the parking lot, still shouting obsceni-ties.

In the end the police escorted me to my car and offered to drive me home. I rode in the squad car with one officer, while another fol-lowed in my car. No one from the mob dared follow us. When we arrived at my house, I thanked the officers and went inside. Ray hadn't seen the policemen, and I didn't tell him how close I had just come to being a victim of violence. He didn't ask why I was home early from a board meeting.

To its credit, the board did vote to change over Key Elementary. Dr. Letson announced, "We will take this issue under advisement and vote on it at a later date." After holding a public hearing, as we had just done, we could legally vote in private to open Key to black stu-dents.

At nearly all our board meetings, some white delegation would come before us to complain. Their school needed a bigger gym, or the parking lot had to be enlarged and paved, or the grounds needed land-scaping. Hearing their words, I'd pull out a few of the tickler cards that I now kept at my seat during meetings. I would then say, "There are Negro schools, like such-and-such, that have been on double ses-sions for nineteen years. How can we build a bigger gym or enlarge a parking lot, when these schools don't even have enough classrooms or current textbooks, like such-and-such? And did you realize that such-and-such high school doesn't have a science lab? I'm sorry, but this is a board of *education*. We've got to fix basic, serious problems like these first."

To say I wasn't a popular member of the board's "team" is an understatement. My outspoken ways resulted in more publicity than anyone in public office needs. My name frequently appeared in newspaper headlines during the early 1960s: "Mrs. Mitchell Rips Negro School Setup"; "Board Member Hits Cost of Keeping Segregation"; "Mrs. Mitchell Raps Church Racial Bias"; "Racial Solution Held Church Job Says Mitchell"; "Convictions Involve Mitchell in Controversy"; "Sports Over-Emphasis Holds Education Back Says Mitchell."

My efforts to reduce the attention paid to sports caused me a great deal of trouble. In April 1963, after carefully studying the school system's budget, I wrote an article for the Sunday magazine of the *Atlanta Journal and Constitution* that was entitled "The High Cost of High School Football." It read in part:

> We are spending $201,624 this year for coaches' salaries. This is more than we have budgeted to purchase new books for all our 154 school libraries. Does this show which we think is the real business of our schools—sports or books? Is turning out trained athletes really our job? We certainly do a better job of rewarding brawn than brains. . . . we spent $32,500 for athletic awards and only a minuscule amount for academic awards. . . . The whole purpose of our schools is education. . . . Parents want the academic program paramount, not the athletic program. They know 95% of their children will have to compete in the future in the field of knowledge, not on the athletic field.

Many readers responded with a few words of their own. The editor of the Sunday magazine told me that he had received over 100 letters from grateful parents and only a few from those who disagreed. He later published the letters, saying that it was a record number for the paper. I gave personal letters that I received to Superintendent Letson so that he could read them. When I asked him on several later occasions to return them, he invariably told me that he hadn't found time to read them yet. All the fellows on the board were mad at me, but with my convictions, how could I remain silent when the problems, both academic and racial, had become overwhelming?

When I voiced my concerns, Dr. Letson accused me of "nit-picking." A mutual friend told me, "John Letson tells me you do a lot of 'nit-picking' at board meetings. John says you bring up a lot of unnecessary items."

I responded, "Do you call double sessions, overcrowded classes, high pupil-teacher ratios, the lack of text and library books, and poor recreational areas of black schools 'nit-picking'?"

"At the last meeting there wasn't time to bring all this up," my friend persisted.

"What would be a good time?" I asked indignantly. "Dr. Letson makes out the agenda for every meeting. He brings up so many items and discusses them at such length that members become exhausted and it gets later and later. I don't want to prolong the meetings, but for God's sake when are board members given any time to speak for the citizens we were elected to represent? All we do is attend Dr. Letson's overly controlled meetings, not our own."

My friend shifted uneasily in his seat. I'm sure he thought he was doing me and Superintendent Letson a favor, but my anger made him uncomfortable. "Tell Dr. Letson," I said, "that he is our employee. He was hired by the board to run the school system, not to run the board. And besides, if he wants to tell me anything, I would appreciate his telling me to my face. I don't like subtle hints from friends, hints that I feel are intended to put me in my place."

I may have been at odds with the superintendent and the members of the board, but the public response to my efforts was encouraging. Mayor Ivan Allen wrote: "I am proud of the job you are doing on the

Atlanta Board of Education, and I am sure you and I agree that getting things done is not always a pleasant task." In 1964, Mayor Allen presented me with one of the city's "Good Neighbor of the Year" awards. W. H. Montague, president of the Georgia AFL-CIO, wrote: "We know of no one better qualified to provide the finest education for our children, or no one more dedicated to getting the job done and NOW."

I especially appreciated Pat Watters's comments in his book *The South and the Nation:*

> In many Southern cities at least one courageous school official sought to counteract the object lesson in sophisticated dishonesty on display before the children. In Atlanta it [was] Sara Mitchell who rose up in one of those moments of wrath that come upon moderate prophets. Parental response was strong enough to get her elected to the school board where she precariously fought with typical members of such a board, mostly businessmen, mostly opposed in spirit to the meaning of real education.

Perhaps the oddest tribute took the form of an invitation. Atlanta has long had a British consulate, and every June there was a lavish celebration of the Queen's birthday at the consul's private residence in old-money Buckhead. Since only the most prominent VIPs in the city's social and business circles were invited, I was surprised and delighted to find one of the handsome engraved invitations in my mailbox. I had been invited as a member of the Board of Education, and so I went alone. I simply told Ray I was going to an education function.

Her Royal Highness would surely have been pleased with the pomp and pageantry. After the guests had assembled on the spacious back lawn, we were served champagne. Then, amid a flurry of drums, the dignified consul appeared on a second-story balcony and greeted us. A flag ceremony followed, and the consul gave a formal speech about the Queen's birthday and the glories of the British Empire. To conclude the ceremony, all the guests sang "God Save the Queen," after which we raised our glasses in the centuries-old toast "Long live the Queen!"

The party then shifted inside the elegant house, where an elaborate buffet table and bar had been set up. As I started looking around, I was surprised to see more and more of my friends, both black and white. I was puzzled. We were not Atlanta's usual VIPs, either socially or in terms of the business power structure.

Two weeks later I found out just how unusual this particular birthday celebration had been. A British friend on the staff at the consulate asked me whether I knew why I had been invited. Then she said, "Well, a new consul arrived a few months ago, and as he looked over the guest list for the Queen's upcoming birthday party, he asked—surely a first for a British consul assigned to Atlanta—'Have any blacks been included?' After a shocked silence, one of his local staff members replied, 'Oh, no, that would never do in Atlanta, not at this level of society.'

" 'Well,' said the consul, 'no blacks, no party.'

"Consternation reigned among the staff. . . . 'There must be a celebration, it's a long-standing tradition,' the consul was told, but he remained adamant, and finally a diplomatic compromise was reached. *Two* parties would be held, one for the prominent, Old South types and another the next night for blacks and whites who were known to enjoy each other's company."

Such were Atlanta's first tentative steps toward integration.

6

Sunday Morning at Ebenezer

In April 1963 I wrote a letter to Martin Luther King, Jr.

Dear Dr. King,

As a member of the Atlanta Board of Education I have just this year finished visiting all of our schools—126 elementary and 28 high schools. Having grown up in Atlanta, this was an eye-opening experience.

Our public schools are "separate" for sure but "equal" is far, far from the truth. Knowing of your concern for fair, equal, improved education for black students, I would like to discuss this important subject with you since I now have a great deal of information.

I will call your office for an appointment at your convenience.

Sincerely,

Sara P. Mitchell

When I saw Dr. King, I told him about my visits to Atlanta schools. White schools, I said, were better designed, more solidly built, with more acreage for playgrounds. They were better landscaped and maintained, with buildings that were better equipped and furnished. Textbooks and library books were more numerous in white schools. I told Dr. King I had noticed that a black school's playground had only one basketball hoop, while a white school had fifteen.

Most telling were the overcrowding and larger class sizes in black schools. At Butler Elementary School, for example, the principal told me, "Our school has been on double sessions for nineteen years."

Dr. King listened intently without interrupting. I felt he was carefully weighing the information, my assessment of it, and me. We had a long, unhurried discussion of the disadvantages of being a black student in the segregated school systems in the South. Martin Luther King of course knew the situation firsthand, having grown up and attended public school in Atlanta. I was merely updating him.

At the end of our visit, I spoke of my conclusion, borne out by my experience, that schools are unequal anywhere they are separate. My visits to every public school in the city of Atlanta had given me all the facts I needed to prove the point.

In parting, Dr. King remarked, "One of the civil rights movement's biggest problems, and our first priority, is securing equal education for black students. Please keep me and the leaders of the movement informed. We must keep in touch."

I very much wanted to keep in touch, but I didn't know how to go about it. By now Dr. King was involved in a multitude of civil rights activities that demanded constant attention. There was a crisis virtually every day. Eventually I decided to attend Ebenezer Baptist Church on Sunday mornings. That way I could hear Dr. King preach and then try to find a few minutes to talk to him after the service. I had heard that wherever he might be during the week, he always came back to preach at his church—unless, of course, he happened to be in jail somewhere!

Ebenezer has a typical Baptist sanctuary that was, and still is, too small for its large congregation. The pews downstairs and in the balcony lacked cushions, and there was very little carpeting. The pulpit is in the center, with the choir seated in back. Above the choir is a stained glass window depicting a lighted cross and Jesus kneeling in prayer. The white interior walls make the atmosphere restful.

While I loved the Sunday morning sermons, I also looked forward to hearing the choir. Some of the younger, newer members obviously preferred to sing classical music, which they had studied. The older members, who made up most of the congregation, preferred spirituals. I know they were Dr. King's favorites. The choir director had evidently reached a compromise. A church bulletin I kept from July 1965 includes works by Dupré, Rigaudon, Ferraro, Cortège, and litany but also "Blessed Assurance" and "Only Trust Him."

The spirituals, when sung in a low, sweet harmony, moved me inexpressibly. I remember feeling tears run down my cheeks as I listened. I often thought that if the choir sang one more beautifully haunting spiritual, I would melt into a huge tear.

There were seldom more than ten or twelve white visitors at Ebenezer when I was there. Most were from out of town even after Dr. King had won the Nobel Peace Prize in December of 1964. I often got calls from out-of-town visitors, and even occasionally an Atlantan, who would say, "I hear you know Dr. King personally. Would you introduce me to him?" And I'd answer, "Gladly, I'll pick you up next Sunday morning and we can go to Ebenezer Baptist Church." I could tell by their voices that this was not the response they wanted. Those who declined missed a rare opportunity. Those who accepted, I am sure, never forgot the experience.

One Sunday I was sitting in the audience with a German visitor who had accepted my invitation. Much to my surprise I heard Reverend King, Sr., say, "I see we have Mrs. Sara Mitchell with us today." He left the pulpit, came down the aisle to where we were, and gave me, as I stood, a great bear hug. The visitor told me later that he changed his views about the South and segregation forever right then and there.

The depth and sincerity of Dr. King's spiritual commitment to the church impressed me even before I heard him preach. This commitment was clearly brought out in his beautifully expressed "Letter from Birmingham Jail." The *Atlanta Journal* published the piece in full—much to the paper's credit, since the year was 1963. The letter had been written in response to white southern clergymen who had joined together to censure the "much too militant action in Birmingham." They pleaded for Dr. King "to go slow; the time is not right. Our people are not ready. Rome was not built in a day."

Deeply moved by the calm logic of Dr. King's answer to the clergymen, and by his letter's compassionate tone, I again wrote to him.

Dear Dr. King,

    I agree with you that the time to "go slow" has long passed. As a lifelong member of the Methodist Church in good standing, I am one of "our people" the clergy spoke for. I want you to know they do not speak for me. The love and truth you so beautifully expressed in your letter went straight to my heart.

He took the time to respond in a letter dated July 25, 1963:

Dear Mrs. Mitchell:

    Thank you for your very kind letter concerning my letter from the Birmingham jail. I am happy to know that you found this epistle helpful. It represented my humble attempt to interpret the meaning of our struggle for freedom and bring moral principles to bear on the difficult problem of racial injustice that pervades our nation. I can assure you that your encouraging words will give me new courage and vigor to carry on in this struggle to make the brotherhood of man a reality and bring the American dream into full realization.

    Let me also take this opportunity to express my deep appreciation for the courageous stand you are taking on the Atlanta School Board for the cause of brotherhood and integration. I appreciate your strong, forthright statements far more than words can express. Under separate cover I am sending you a copy of my new book entitled *Strength to Love*.

Sincerely yours,
Martin Luther King, Jr.

Preaching was not Dr. King's first career choice. He had thought of becoming a lawyer or a doctor. Even though his maternal grandfather and his father were ministers, he found the Negro church too sensational. He was repelled when he saw members speaking in tongues, and he disliked rabid fundamentalists. In his youth, he also felt that the church lacked social relevance. He formed a new concept of the ministry, however, under the influence of his mentor, Benjamin E. Mays, then president of Morehouse College.

Dr. King's sermons were always in plain English that could easily be understood. They were seldom of a personal nature, but one Sunday, I recall him telling the congregation how he and his family had been harassed. He said that their lives had been threatened by a late night telephone call, that he was almost ready to give up, and that he had tried to think of a way to move out of the picture without being a coward. He added that he had prayed to God to give him the strength to go on, to have the courage to face whatever it would take to become the leader his people needed.

I attended Ebenezer on many Sundays. I became a great admirer of Dr. King's sermons, both for their content and for his style of delivery. Their message was always helpful as well as spiritual. They were carefully thought-out, masterful appeals to reason. Dr. King did not do battle with sinners or even preach against sin as such. He preached sermons of love, sermons to encourage the timid of heart to be courageous, sermons to give the downtrodden self-confidence. To those who felt inferior he said, "Hold your head high, for you are the sons and daughters of the living God."

Dr. King didn't wave his arms about or shout or pace nervously back and forth in front of the podium like so many present-day evangelists. He didn't tell jokes. There were no visual or physical distractions to detract from the power of his words.

Dr. King's sermons were about loving your enemies, loving your neighbor whoever and wherever he was. They were about justice, freedom, and the need for a peaceful world. He stressed the nobility of man and man's power to right wrongs and correct evils in a non-violent way. I always left Ebenezer after his sermons feeling renewed in spirit and resolved to live a more loving, caring, giving life.

One sermon I particularly remember dealt with "acceptance." Dr. King told the congregation not to accept the unacceptable. Blacks in particular had long been told to accept their role in life. Instead he said, "God did not want Rosa Parks to accept standing in the back of the bus in order to let a white person sit down. God wants Rosa Parks to sit down right now, right now on this earth."

For centuries blacks had been told to "accept the unacceptable" so that they could go to Heaven, walk through the pearly gates, and "eat at the welcome table." Dr. King wanted none of that.

Like the biblical prophets of the Old Testament, Dr. King had the courage to proclaim truth and justice as he believed it. As early as October 8, 1958, in the *Christian Century,* he wrote, "Not every minister can be a prophet but some must be prepared for the ordeals of this high calling and be willing to suffer courageously for righteousness. May the problems of race in America soon make hearts burn so the prophets will rise up, saying, 'Thus said the Lord' and cry out as Amos did, 'Let justice roll down like waters, and righteousness like an ever flowing stream.'"

Dr. King himself of course became just such a prophet. He was first and foremost a preacher, not an activist. In the end, because of his religious convictions, he felt he had no choice but to take action. In his mind it wasn't what a man stood for but what he did about it that counted. In his words what counted most was "not where one stands in moments of comfort and convenience" (as in the pulpit) but "where one stands at times of challenge and controversy" (as in the civil rights battles).

Dr. King's choice of the ministry as a career, and also as a "calling," gave him the perfect platform as he sought to bring Jesus' message to bear on the social evils of his day. His words, spoken with strong in-

tellectual and spiritual conviction and often with righteous indignation, were soon to be heard around the world. Words without action,
however, were not part of Dr. King's thinking. Like Gandhi, he believed in demonstrations. "There is nothing," he said, "more powerful
than the tramp, tramp, tramp of marching feet."

History will record that Dr. King, by his leadership and his example,
caused millions of blacks to seek and gain full rights of citizenship.
Many blacks who once lived in crushing, degrading poverty in back
alleys, shacks, and slums are now successful business and professional
people. Blacks, once not allowed the right to vote, are now holding
elected public office in city, county, and state.

When someone asks me how I feel about Martin Luther King, I
have a hard time answering. To me he was a present-day Moses, a
leader who inspired millions to follow his nonviolent revolution. He
was a liberator not only of the black race but of my white race as well.
He believed in trying love as a tool, in loving your fellow man into
doing what was right. Through his words and his deeds, Dr. King
caused millions of people to reexamine their humanity.

In 1969, on the anniversary of his birth, I wrote about him in a
letter to the editor of the *Atlanta Constitution*:

Dr. King was a gentle, quiet man but when he spoke, the truth
of his words shook the conscience of a nation.

His voice was soft but the rhythm, the cadence, the power of it
rose to a mighty crescendo that thrilled and inspired a multitude.

Dr. King was small of stature but he feared no man. He lived
by his belief that "what strength we lack God will provide."

He cared deeply for all mankind while knowing that millions
of white people hated him, hated him with a passion destructive
to themselves.

Dr. King was kind and thoughtful and forgiving to his friends
and his enemies.

Those who knew him knew he died without hate, died without a grudge, died with a love for all mankind. Millions were against him yet he overcame them all, even in death.

I came to know Dr. King better as the months of 1963 and 1964 passed. The press paid little attention when he first moved to Atlanta, but soon there were screaming front-page headlines noting his every move. Through church services and numerous civil rights meetings I came to know Coretta well and saw her often as a personal friend. I also knew Dr. King's family, his mother and father, his brother, A. D., and his sister, Christine.

In Atlanta Martin Luther King's father is aptly and affectionately known as "Daddy" King, the patriarch who held everything together— his family, his church, and his community. I became good friends with Daddy King, as we often attended the same civil rights meetings. I also heard him preach on the Sundays when Martin Luther King, Jr., was away from the city.

I never knew a more loving, outgoing, warm human being than Daddy King. I did hear, however, that he ruled his home like an Old Testament patriarch. When the children broke a rule or became sassy or sullen, Daddy took a strap to them. No doubt that was the way he was raised. His grandparents had been slaves, his father a sharecropper and his mother a cleaning woman. He turned to the ministry and came to Atlanta from the farm in 1917. Although he began his education in the fifth grade as an adult, he finished high school and later entered Morehouse College.

Like his son Martin, Reverend King believed that the church should not only speak to the souls of its members but to the needs of the community in which they lived. "Religion should be evident in the market place," he said, "as well as inside the gates of the church." I knew firsthand that he practiced what he preached.

In the 1930s Daddy King was a member of the Executive Board of the local branch of the NAACP. It was a time when many whites regarded the organization as dangerously radical. He led several hundred blacks in a voting rights march on Atlanta's City Hall in 1936. It was something "no living soul in the city had ever seen." Along with other black leaders he fought for years for the integration of the police force, a goal that was accomplished in 1948, although blacks could not arrest whites until 1962.

Reverend King, despite his own contributions to society, gave all the credit to his son and to the Lord. Martin Luther King, Jr., received the Nobel Peace Prize in Oslo, Norway, on December 10, 1964. Two nights earlier, Reverend King had said, "I always wanted to make a contribution, and all you got to do if you wanted to contribute, you got to ask the Lord, and let him know. The Lord heard me, and in some special kind of way I don't even know how, he came down through Georgia and laid his hand on me and my wife and he gave us Martin Luther King, Jr., and our prayers were answered and when my head is cold and my bones are bleached, the King family will go down in world history because Martin King is a Nobel Prize winner."

Reverend King was pastor of Ebenezer for forty-four years. He was a God-fearing man who preached straight from his heart in plain everyday English. You felt that he was preaching right to you and that God was listening to every word.

7

Not the Best of Times

The year 1964 was unsettling. President Kennedy had been assassinated in late November of 1963. As 1964 began, people were still in shock. During his first State of the Union address, President Johnson unveiled his ambitious "War on Poverty" and called for passage of a sweeping, tough civil rights bill.

In Atlanta, police arrested seventy-eight demonstrators on January 18 in a confrontation at a segregated Krystal restaurant. White flight was increasing in many of Atlanta's Southside neighborhoods. Schools were always being caught in the crossfire. Consequently, a number of board meetings were spent deciding how and when to change over certain schools. The city's desegregation plan was being challenged in federal court. Every board member knew that the plan would soon be thrown out. What would we do next? Realistically speaking, the federal courts were probably going to tell *us* what the next desegregation plan would be.

My job on the board was full time, but I didn't work on board business every Monday through Friday from 8:30 to 5:30. The board was the centerpiece around which everything else revolved, but it was equally my passport to a number of other liberal and civic efforts.

For Christmas of 1963 one of my best friends had given me a red leather, legal-size "Standard Daily Journal." On the flyleaf it bore the inscription: "To Sara. With all the interesting experiences you are having, you should keep a journal." For the next year I dutifully wrote in that red leather journal every day. On a deeply personal level, I felt in such turmoil about my marriage that I thought writing down my feelings might help me sort them out. In the end I wrote about many other things as well. Below are some of my entries. My comments on them today appear in brackets.

January 5. Ray has become even more resentful of my political life, especially my liberal-radical leanings. I have become increasingly aware of a serious undertow of disaffection. I never tell him what I do during the day, where I go, or with whom, nor does he ever ask, I guess because he doesn't want to face the controversial public life I lead. Instead we discuss what proper, traditional husbands deem appropriate—social events and engagements, friends, sports, food, and church activities, plus any acceptable activities of our three children, now grown. I am proud that two of the three are as "liberal" as I am.

[In fact, I was recently reminded of a little time-saving strategy I devised that reveals just how separate my public and married lives had become by 1964. Ray left the house promptly at 8:05 every morning, when I'd be rinsing the breakfast dishes to put in the dishwasher (we no longer had a maid daily). As soon as I heard the front door close, I knew I could swing into action—I figured out that evening's supper menu, went back into the breakfast room, and set the table for that night. In this way, I knew I could be away from home as long as possible. All I had to do was be back by five to begin fixing the meal. It saddens me now to realize how totally apart Ray and I had grown by then.]

January 15. Now that the children are away from home, every day is mine to plan and use as the need arises. I don't know how many other wives would admit this, but life is really easy for us with all our labor-saving appliances and at least part-time help. I can have the house in order, the bed made, and the dishes in the dishwasher in less than an hour's time. Cooking has been greatly overrated as a skill. Anyone with minimum brains can prepare a good meal in an hour's time.

I see red when men repeat that old saying "A woman's place is in the home." What are women supposed to do after the children have been raised?

February 12. My mother and mother-in-law are both like my husband in one way: they don't approve of my social or political life. The other day when I picked up my mother so that we could attend a social affair of hers, she took one look and said, "I didn't think you'd be wearing a hat, and I want you to. I've put all my hats on the bed. Choose one." I dutifully put one on and we left. I knew then that the way she wanted me to be—a properly dressed, socially prominent matron—wasn't me at all.

My mother-in-law let me know of her disapproval when I stopped by on my way home from town today. She was reading the evening paper. My picture happened to be on the front page under the heading "Mitchell Rips Negro School Set Up." She put the paper aside and said in her quiet voice, "How are you, dear?" Then she asked about the children. During all the years I have been active in the civil rights movement and on the school board, she has never mentioned any of these activities to me.

March 15. I had an appointment with a couple who had recently moved to Atlanta and wanted to see me. Their problem? They were considering buying a house in upscale Ansley Park and had heard that the neighborhood was changing because some underprivileged children had been admitted to the nearby Spring Street School. Would the Atlanta school board take steps to see that the property this couple wanted to buy did not decline in value under these circumstances?

I told them that schools cannot be run to keep neighborhoods exclusive. And yes, there were some underprivileged people attending Spring Street. You will have to take your chances with property values.

This couple's attitude made me wonder what had happened to our supposedly democratic society that had made them want to come in contact with only their own kind.

March 20. Meeting of "Partners for Progress" this morning. This is an organization working for an orderly integration of the schools. When schools open this fall we are going to have, by federal law, a greatly increased number of black students in white schools. The Partners know that the majority of white parents, pupils, and teachers, as well as the public, are not "ready," and they are doing what they can to set a climate of acceptance.

Liberals are so at home by now in the company of black friends and coworkers in the movement—meeting and eating and enjoying each others' company—that we have to remind ourselves not to be too hard on those we are trying to "bring along."

March 21. I wanted to discuss some of our increasingly serious marital problems with Ray tonight, but he said he was not in the mood. He never wants to talk, so what can I do? Can a marriage exist with no words, no understanding of what is in the other's heart?

March 22. I can't figure Ray out. After the unpleasantness of last night he was as agreeable today as though nothing had happened. What kind of cover-up or forgetfulness is this? Sometimes I think he doesn't remember a word I say, then again I think he remembers but believes in a way of life that excludes any unpleasantness—the "don't mention it and it will go away" school of thought. I don't subscribe to this. I believe one should discuss problems that lead to unhappiness and try to solve them, not ignore them.

How much and how long can we keep covering up?

It isn't that Ray objects to my being away from home so often. He objects to the fact that what I do is not on the "socially approved" list of what company executives' wives are supposed to do. Many of the approved activities are nothing more than time killers and status symbols. I need my energy and my time for the important things in life like brotherhood, peace, and justice for all, now especially. Besides, there is no way I can go back to the socially accepted proper "Southern Way of Life." It is much too late.

March 25. I am on a committee to entertain foreign visitors to the city. Today I was asked to take two white Afrikaners to lunch and to visit our schools. The visitors especially wanted to hear what the churches were doing to ease the school integration crisis. I told them nothing much except for a few inspired members and ministers. According to the southern church, segregation is sanctioned by God and the Bible.

March 31. I attended the forty-fourth annual meeting of the Atlanta League of Women Voters this morning. There is no way I can separate myself as a politician from the League. As valuable as the knowledge and political know-how I've gained is the influence of League members on me, intelligent women working to be of service to their city and the nation. They have made a priceless contribution to my life!

April 16. Ray and I disagree on the church's role in the civil rights movement. We disagree on the race problem, on women and their role in society. We disagree on finances (he keeps ours to himself). Living under the strain and stress of constant disagreement and disapproval is wearing me out.

Ray believes in holding on and covering up. I believe in facing up. The struggle is becoming quietly maddening. What to do, when, and how? Would the cure, divorce, be worse than the problem?

May 6. Quite a day for Georgia. President Lyndon B. Johnson and his daughter, Lynda Bird, spent a day and night here on a "poverty" tour. There was much media excitement, but I did not even get to watch it on TV. I was attending a breakfast at Kirkwood School just when the motorcade was going down Peachtree Street. At least I shouldn't feel too bad. I was where the real action should have taken place. Kirkwood Elementary is in the poverty category for sure.

May 10. Tonight I attended the PTA's president's Council of Greater Atlanta, which is all white. The featured speaker, a young attractive minister who looked like Billy Graham, said nothing of any significance. A few stale, pointless jokes, a few tried and true rules to live by. Just what the audience seemed to expect and want. If there are any educators or PTAs in Atlanta now that are fired up about better education and more nearly equal education for all students, I have not heard of them.

A pox on the PTA. A recent article in the *Saturday Evening Post* called the PTA a "completely ineffectual, meaningless group, one not facing up to any real problems of the day." About like the southern church, I thought.

May 12. At 3:00 I spoke to a group of teachers in training at Spelman College on the Atlanta University campus. My answers to questions about tenure aroused hostility. I said I thought that our teacher tenure policies were too lenient, that many unqualified teachers were allowed to teach. I told the teachers that the Atlanta board had never let a teacher go for any reason apart from "moral turpitude."

May 18. I found out today that even Ralph McGill has become a dirty word. At the dressmaker's being fitted for a new summer dress I mentioned the publisher of the *Atlanta Constitution* and felt the sharp jab of a pin. To forestall any more jabs, I mentioned that I knew McGill because he was a Sigma Chi fraternity brother of my husband's. My explanation was apparently acceptable, and the fitting proceeded with no further pain.

May 30. I was invited to speak to Local 20 of the AFL-CIO this noon. Local 20 is the union of custodians, maids, and cafeteria workers in the school system. After studying our budget, I found their salaries disgracefully low. For what little help I could offer the union members were so grateful that I felt terrible. I promised to mention their need for a pay increase again at the next board meeting, and I reminded them to have a delegation on hand.

June 2. A mother of a high school graduate called me. She is Jewish. Her problem was the baccalaureate sermon preached by the minister of my old church, Peachtree Road Methodist. She complained that it was an evangelical, "only through Christ will you be saved" sermon. She thought this was inappropriate and wrong. So do I, especially after all the feeling over the school prayer decision. I am opposed to any teaching, praying, or sermonizing that separates one human being from another.

June 3. If our long marriage fails, the hardest part for me would be giving up our house that I have put so much loving care into. I feel sure that Ray would never volunteer to leave.

How I would miss my beautiful, pale blue bedroom with its big picture window looking out on a forest of green. Then there is the back deck overlooking the yard where our children played and the winding, rocky creek below. On warm summer mornings we ate breakfast on the deck and lingered over coffee and the morning paper. How could I leave all this for a small cramped apartment with possibly no view, no deck, no porch? Alone I could never afford a house like ours.

Can one just dismiss these pleasures as material blessings, or are they the very basis of one's joy of life?

June 5. To Capitol Avenue School in one of Atlanta's poorest neighborhoods to give out diplomas to the eighth grade graduation class. I stood on the stage and smiled into the students' happy faces as I handed them the small rolled-up piece of parchment. Graduations are always a proud and special time for students and their parents. This is especially true of black parents. For me, however, this turned out to be a surprisingly unhappy experience. These young children already looked defeated by life. Their undernourished, poorly clothed bodies showed years of poverty, bad diets, and lack of medical care. Their sad, dark, haunting eyes contradicted their smiles.

God! What have we done, what are we doing, to these children? How can southerners say, "I don't feel any guilt when it comes to blacks? No guilt for starvation wages, backbreaking work, indifference to their needs? No guilt for outright cruelty and years of humiliating servitude? No guilt?

June 13. A group of seven white teachers from all over the United States have come here under the sponsorship of the Mennonites' Community Service to teach in our summer school programs. They will receive free room and board but no salary. They are staying at the Mennonite house, which is located in one of Atlanta's poorest black neighborhoods. These volunteers will be the first white teachers to teach in a black school—if they can get permission, that is.

Reverend Vincent Harding asked me to be the go-between for them because of a school board policy that no white teacher could teach in a black school and vice versa. I told Vincent I would make a special appeal to Letson. After hearing me out, Letson said he would give permission as long as I kept quiet about it.

This afternoon I spent two hours talking with the teachers and answering questions about the schools and the city and what they could expect. We had a delightful time together.

June 30. Although I dread the thought of divorce I dread just as much a life where two people antagonize each other, become quarrelsome, where there is jealousy and resentment, where both feel bound, unable to be themselves, where they feel unappreciated, unloved.

What claim does one's family have on one after the children are grown? Is my own life important enough to inconvenience the lives of my family? On the other hand, if a person stays miserable for the sake of others, how long can they go on without *everyone's* becoming miserable?

July 1. What I worried about in the small hours of a sleepless night is hard to recapture in the morning. I do remember one thing. If we divorced, how could I bear to face a life of loneliness? The last vestiges of my mind run the gauntlet throughout the long night while I wait for daylight, a cup of coffee, and the security of another day's rewarding activity.

July 5. I finished reading *Teenage Tyranny* today. The author stated that adults have turned over their authority, but not the benefit of their experience, to teenagers, also that parents are lax, permissive, place too much emphasis on the social, recreational, athletic side of life—that teachers are trying too hard to make learning "fun." [This is in 1964, remember! The more things change, the more they stay the same.]

Even if somewhat exaggerated, there is considerable truth to the author's premise. I agree that a harmful aftermath of the affluent society is too much indulgence and too little expectation of our teenagers. The "popularity" cult deserves a large part of the blame. Our daughters must be beautiful and desirable, our sons successful and rich; all in the approved Madison Avenue, *Vogue* and *Forbes* magazine way. Our goals for our children are next to atrocious.

July 10. I attended a large tea this afternoon given for a bride-to-be. The hostess's house on Tuxedo Road was "Old South," from the box-wood lined driveway to the handsome crystal chandelier over the highly polished mahogany dining room table to the heavy satin draperies at the long, floor-to-ceiling windows.

The guests were all well dressed, well educated, and relatively wealthy. Greetings among us went something like this: "Hello, Sara, how are you? How is Ray? How are your children? How have you been?" These words are repeated some twenty times, with no one really hearing or caring to hear your answer. Somehow I manage these affairs with the proper social grace, long taught me by my family. I smile, answer all questions in the approved manner. The real me is something else! I have often gone from a civil rights meeting of the NAACP on Auburn Avenue to one of these parties in Buckhead. What a tug-of-war my mind and my heart endure.

July 12. At the school board meeting tonight, we spent the whole evening talking about buildings. If only I could have one-tenth the time to talk about education. Almost forgotten, unspoken are words like "curriculum" and "instruction."

July 27. At two o'clock I went to the YWCA to meet with a group of native Africans who are touring America this summer. I was asked to speak on integration in the Atlanta schools and then to answer questions. Everything I said had to be translated—a slow, tedious process. These encounters with foreigners are difficult and mentally wearing. I suppose foreigners feel the same way when we visit them. I always feel rewarded, however, after the sessions are over.

Sometimes in small ways I have the feeling I have helped cement the bonds of brotherhood around the world. A dark African, dressed in yards of draped material, thong sandals on his feet, looked me straight in the eye at one point. We smiled, connecting and communicating with one another perfectly.

August 2. I began a new book tonight, *Nietzsche* by Walter Kaufmann. At this point in my life I find *Nietzsche* exciting reading. For example: "If you wish to strive for peace of soul and pleasure, then believe: If you wish to be a devotee of truth, then inquire."

August 15. The school budget couldn't cover summer school classes for the pupils who need it—the deprived from poor families—so I raised the fifteen-dollar tuition for about eighty children by asking my friends for donations. At one school I met a mother who had nine children with no real husband or father for any of them. These kids seem to have little or no chance of making it. The remarkable thing is that many of them do make it.

September 8. One unusual school case I have been working on involves a seven-year-old white boy whose parents want to send him to the nearest school, which happens to be black. When the parents got in touch with the school principal, he expressed alarm and went to the area superintendent, Dr. Hillard Bowen. Bowen told the parents that the grade their son wanted to enter was not yet integrated, so the parents called me. I contacted Letson, who said he would tell Bowen to let their child attend the school of his choice. The parents thanked me profusely.

September 15. At last night's school board meeting we heard protests from the white parents at the recently integrated West Fulton High School. There were jeers, stomps, and boos throughout the meeting. I cringed at first, then said to myself, "You are a duly elected public official, so sit straight, think clearly, and act the part. Do not be intimidated."

Unlike the parents, two spokesmen—one from the NAACP and one from the Atlanta Council of Human Relations—presented their argument for the integration of the school in an orderly, reasonable manner. Quite a contrast to the riled-up parents.

According to school attendance records, about 200 white students at West Fulton are staying out of class. Most of the other white students moved from their old neighborhoods during the summer. The last figures on enrollment show 1,038 blacks and 348 whites. Before integration there were 1,300 white students.

As upsetting as the integration of white schools became for schools and neighborhoods, there were two great advantages for black students and their families. The students now have many badly needed additional classrooms, and black families can now buy houses that are just as badly needed—houses vacated by the white families.

September 20. Philosophy and religion as well as politics are implicated in the upcoming election between Lyndon Johnson and Barry Goldwater. In my mind the Republicans stand for "What's mine is mine and I am going to keep it," while the Democrats say, "What's mine is mine and I am willing to share it."

Republicans in the South think Goldwater will restore states' rights, which they understand to mean every black back in his or her place—preferably back in the cotton fields or in the kitchens of the "white folks."

October 2. My old problem is back: should Ray and I divorce? I still can't make the final decision. Who knows the pain, the difficulties of going through a divorce after thirty years of marriage? Love, the real reason for any marriage, in our case is dead. Nothing but duty is left. How long can you live in the same house with anything that is dead, even for duty's sake?

I worry about how to separate our belongings. Who gets what? Who gets the family scrapbooks full of baby pictures and happier times? Who gets the china and silver? And how can you give up a house you have come to love after all these years? Give up a kitchen that is perfect to work in and the view from my picture window and the back deck overlooking the deep woods? Give up my nice, friendly neighbors? Are these reasons enough to stay married?

October 20. This morning I picked up a visitor from the Netherlands who is visiting here and wanted to observe some public schools. Mrs. Van Hooften-Hoof turned out to be attractive and interesting, a member of Parliament and a lawyer. She asked to see some new school buildings, also some schools attended by blacks, so I took her to our showplaces, Harper High and Oglethorpe Elementary. Afterward I asked if she would like to eat lunch at Pascal's, a longtime favorite with civil rights workers. She was delighted, even anxious, to have this experience. At the restaurant I saw many of my white friends and black friends, including John Yungblut, the head of Quaker House, and Frances Pauley of the Georgia Council of Human Relations. Mrs. Van Hooften-Hoof told me she found the mix of races there extremely enlightening.

Tonight I was invited to sit on the platform with Senator Herman Talmadge at a meeting of the Henry Grady High PTA. Although I have never been an admirer of his, he spoke well on education. At least he and I have that interest in common.

I took a visitor from Sweden with me who wanted to know more about our educational system. Later he told me he was surprised and perplexed by the proceedings. "Those long passages from the Bible which were read, and the lengthy opening prayer—do PTAs always do this?" he asked.

"Always," I answered, "without fail. Forget the Supreme Court prayer decision down here. You are in the Bible Belt."

November 7. Went to a school board meeting and breakfast with the area superintendents to discuss problems of integration. Our grade-a-year plan, which has been in effect for the past few years, must, according to the federal court, be speeded up next year. An agreement was reached to integrate kindergarten and the first grade. We still spend most of our time discussing the problem of race rather than education. I guess it will take twenty years before we stabilize enrollments. Maybe I am too optimistic, but I still believe that I will live to see the day when people are judged, not by the color of their skin, or their nationality, or their sex, but by their character.

November 19. Saint James Methodist Church [my church in 1964] is having "Five Great Nights for God," according to the church bulletin. What about all the other days and nights? I wondered. I know a lot of things I could do for God if only I would. I could feed the hungry, clothe the naked, visit the prisons, minister to the sick and lonely, shelter the homeless. I know what I could do, all right, but none of them includes going to Saint James for five nights and listening to irrelevant, uninspiring sermons.

November 21. I met my close friend Dorothy Gibson and Curtis Henson, a school administrator, for lunch to talk over the proposal for use of funds under the Economic Opportunity Act. The proposal was presented at the last board meeting. I raised several questions about how the funds are to be administered, meaning how fairly, and got the proposal postponed until we had time to look into the matter further. I am for the proposal, I think, but I resent the way it was presented to the board members—as a $928,000 expenditure with no time for discussion. Letson often takes it for granted that we will vote on issues that he has taken no pains or time to brief us on. It makes me very angry.

I shudder to think of all the fiscal business for which I am ultimately responsible as an elected official, business that I know absolutely nothing about. Board members are apt to be the last, not the first, in the school system to know what is going on financially.

Understanding the school budget is the hardest single task for a board member, yet money lies at the very heart of the school system. I have often been told, "Board members are not expected to understand the budget. It's too complicated." I have also been told that we are not qualified to speak on instructional or curriculum matters. If so, why do we have a board of education?

November 29. Up and out early to a regional workshop put on by the Atlanta Urban League. I was asked to lead one of the sections. The main complaint was how governmental bodies select people to serve on committees. Blacks complained that they were left off the very committees that create the programs and the policies designed to benefit them. I knew just how they felt. Women are left off committees that concern us as well.

I have found that you are appointed to a committee in accordance with some kind of mysterious buddy system or because of the prestige of your name or position. Your ability to think constructively, and your knowledge of, or commitment to, the issues at hand, seem to merit no consideration. To put it simply, you have to "know Joe" or be "somebody." Those named to committees, more often than not, have no real interest in the subject to be dealt with and are usually too busy to attend, let alone contribute or become active.

December 31. As I look back over 1964, the biggest disappointment was my membership on the board. It was an uphill battle all the way. The other members constantly made me feel the "odd member out." And I still haven't resolved my problem at home.

In October 1964 we learned that Martin Luther King, Jr., had been awarded the Nobel Peace Prize. To my knowledge, no Atlantan had ever been recognized with an international honor even remotely as prestigious.

The city, especially the white power structure—generally perceived as "moderate"—was dumbstruck. Our business leaders didn't know how to react. In December, a "planning group" consisting of cultural leaders such as the Most Reverend Paul J. Hallinan, Roman Catholic archbishop of Atlanta; Ralph McGill, publisher of the *Atlanta Constitution;* Benjamin Mays, president of Morehouse College; and Rabbi Jacob M. Rothschild of The Temple decided to hold a banquet honoring King. The planning group included not one business leader.

As described by the *New York Times* for January 23, 1965:

A hometown banquet honoring the Rev. Dr. Martin Luther King Jr., which provoked behind-the-scenes controversy in Atlanta business circles when it was proposed, has won overwhelming public endorsement. . . .

After plans for the dinner were disclosed, just before Christmas, it appeared to have the sponsorship of a number of religious, educational and other Atlanta leaders. Opinions varied, however, among leading businessmen who had been asked to be sponsors.

A spokesman for the planning group said today, however, that although a number of these had declined the use of their names as sponsors many had purchased the $6.50 [!] tickets to attend. . . .

Mr. Don McEvoy, who is coordinating arrangements for the dinner, said that 101 Atlanta citizens had agreed to serve as sponsors of the event. About three-fourths of these are white, he said. He estimated that at least 800 of the 1,400 ticket purchasers were white.

The sponsors' list includes many of the city's most prominent people, with a stronger representation of political leaders than some observers had expected.

Mayor Ivan Allen Jr. and William B. Hartsfield, a former Mayor, are on the list. . . .

The list also includes Vice Mayor Sam Massell Jr., a Democrat; two city aldermen, Rodney Cook and Richard Freeman, both

Republicans, and Mrs. G. Ray Mitchell, a member of the Atlanta Board of Education. All are white. . . .

I was of course more than happy to be a sponsor of an event honoring a man whom I admired tremendously and whom I considered a personal friend. As a sponsor, I had only to agree to have my name publicized (ironically, Ray's name was used, except in the program, where I managed to get myself identified as Mrs. Sara Mitchell).

The city's white power mongers remained reluctant to embrace this obviously integrated event. They did so because, at a hush-hush meeting he convened, J. Paul Austin, chief executive officer of Coca-Cola, told business leaders in no uncertain terms that it was embarrassing for Coca-Cola to be located in a city that was reluctant to honor a Nobel Prize winner. Within two hours of the meeting, every ticket had been sold!

I never discussed the banquet with Ray. On the big night, I dressed in my best cobalt blue cocktail dress, left the house without saying where I was going, and drove downtown to the Dinkler Plaza Hotel. As the dinner got under way, I sat with friends at one of the large tables for ten.

The introductions of King were naturally effusive, and I never was more pleased to be part of a standing ovation. King's remarks were eloquent and moving, as always. I remember thinking that Atlanta had at last done the right thing, that we—black and white together, in the heart of the South—were celebrating together and that all the world would see.

In a narrower sense, but one no less important to me, the event also forced the city's white power structure once and for all to acknowledge formally and very publicly Dr. King's accomplishments in his struggle for justice.

By 1965, I was spending more time going to national education conferences. Atlanta's violence-free desegregation was something people wanted to hear more about. I was a logical choice as speaker because I had experience with this achievement, a background in the League of Women Voters, and a reputation as the only liberal member of the city's school board.

In July alone, I attended Harvard University's annual summer school conference, the St. Paul meeting of the National School Board Association, and—most special of all—the White House Conference on Education, to which only about 200 school board members from across America had been invited. A reception was held at the White House, which I visited for the first time, and I felt an overpowering sense of history. President Johnson and Vice President Humphrey made their visitors feel that by bettering education in each of our towns and cities, we could help America remain competitive and retain its position of world leadership. The tacit message was that if we failed, America would also fail.

By September, too, my marital problems had come to a head. I was at last prepared for divorce. To face divorce after thirty years of marriage takes courage, especially when there is no one, or even the hope of anyone, to fill the void. I had known for some years that my marriage was dead, but I had lacked the courage to end it. Instead, night after sleepless night, I had lain awake, reviewing my fears.

As I recall this time in my life today, more than thirty years later, I am once again aware that all of Ray's hostility centered on my open, active support of the civil rights movement. How different my life from age forty on would have been if I had not become a civil rights activist! Yet I know that I could never have lived differently. None of us can truly feel good about ourselves if we don't honor our deepest convictions.

Whatever may have caused the demise of my marriage, I knew in 1965 that it could not be salvaged. The time had come to leave Ray, no matter what the cost. Ray had long since placed some stock in my name to reduce our taxes. When I decided on divorce, I saw a lawyer and determined that the dividends from that stock, which was legally mine, would allow me to live modestly in an apartment and maintain a car. My salary as a part-time member of the school board was certainly of little help. In 1965 it was all of $300 a month.

I found an apartment less than a mile from our house, in familiar surroundings, with neighbors and friends nearby. It was on the second floor, overlooking grass and trees. I signed a one-year lease, but weeks passed before I could tell Ray that I would be leaving him. As luck would have it, an acquaintance spared me the task. She had seen me enter the apartment the day I rented it. When she called one night after dinner, Ray answered the phone. I heard him say, "What building? We aren't moving anywhere."

I moved out on September 7, 1965, coincidentally the day when I learned that I had won the September 6 primary by a large majority. I was then fifty-three years old, with three married children, three grandchildren, and a part-time job. In the primary election I had had virtually no opposition and had even returned a campaign contribution of seventy-five dollars, explaining to the donor that I had not needed to spend it.

Helen Bullard, my friend the political expert, had been right. She had said, "Don't worry, Sara, you'll get reelected. Voters like honest, outspoken candidates even if they don't always agree with them."

8

From Southern Wrongs to Civil Rights

If there were voters in Atlanta who disagreed with me, there were of course also many elected leaders in the South of the 1960s with whom I, as a voter, scarcely agreed.

George Wallace in his inaugural speech as governor of Alabama in 1962 said, "In the name of the greatest people that ever trod this earth, I draw the line in the dust and throw the gauntlet at the feet of tyranny, and I say, segregation now, segregation tomorrow and segregation forever."

While Wallace was governor, in the words of author Dan Carter, "a barely repressed savagery reigned in Alabama, a day-in, day-out viciousness that permeated the police agencies. Wallace's fixation on real or imagined enemies led to the opening of files on numerous black and liberal organizations. To be black, and to speak even timidly for civil rights, was to throw yourself into twilight world in Alabama."

Wallace and a host of other southern politicians wanted to keep blacks in bondage forever, or so it seemed from their speeches. Lester Maddox, once the governor of Georgia, also came into office through race-hating tactics. Ernest Vandiver, the "No, not one" governor of Georgia who later quietly disappeared from public view, did run for the U.S. Senate but lost in the primary race to Sam Nunn. Roy Harris

was once the powerful speaker of the Georgia Senate and a rabid segregationist. Later, ironically, he became a city attorney in Augusta,
Georgia, serving under a black mayor.

Herman Talmadge was quoted in the *Congressional Record* for June
17, 1964, as saying:

> Mr. President, it has become painfully apparent that in just a
> matter of days the most vicious legislation since the dark days of
> Reconstruction will be forced upon the American people. With
> the passage of this misnamed civil rights bill, individual liberty
> in the United States will be dealt a severe blow. Although I cannot
> describe or suppress the repugnance I feel for this legislation,
> there is no doubt that it will be passed by the Congress, and
> thereafter signed into law by the President. . . . this bill was
> conceived in intemperance and hatred. It was born of lawless
> radical agitation and nurtured by mob violence. I submit that this
> bill is the offspring of a dangerous popular philosophy. . . .
>
> It is my belief that not only the South, but the entire Nation—
> all of the people—will rue the day that this legislation was en-
> acted. The people have been sold a bill of goods. They have been
> caught up in a whirlwind of emotional confusion. . . . they have
> been coerced and intimidated.

Senator Richard B. Russell, speaking before the Eighty-eighth Congress on June 17, 1963, said, "The highest office in the land should
symbolize respect of the law. The South has its shortcomings as well
as other areas, but a calculated campaign waged by the metropolitan
press, television and radio has magnified the unfortunate occurrences
in the South while crimes of violence in other areas have been mini-
mized. This has generated bitterness and hatred against the white
people of the Southern states almost amounting to a national disease."

One hot, summer Sunday afternoon I agreed to go to see Senator
Russell at his home in Winder, Georgia, a small town some thirty

miles from Atlanta. One of the many liberal groups to which I belonged had made an appointment to ask him to vote against closing all of Georgia's public schools rather than integrating them.

Senator Russell was a bachelor who lived in his family home, a prim and neat two-story wooden farmhouse at the end of a dirt driveway. His mother greeted us at the door. She was a frail, thin farm woman who looked as old-fashioned as her house. The living room was sparsely furnished and painfully neat. Fresh glass curtains hung from windows that had been closed to keep out the summer sun.

Our group—all of us white and nervous—waited for the senator in silence. Our spokesman said his piece and made our case. Senator Russell reiterated his opposition to federal intervention and *Brown v. Board of Education*.

In his bid for the presidency in 1952, Senator Russell assured the American black (in a broadcast on "Meet the Press"), "You have nothing to fear from me." His own words notwithstanding, he was king of the filibuster and the embodiment of southern resistance to the emerging civil rights movement.

How difficult it is to forget and forgive the harm inflicted by these politicians before, during, and after the civil rights movement of the 1960s. As Meg Greenfield observed in "How We Shred the Past," in the October 5, 1987, issue of *Newsweek,*

> There is an affliction that is particularly widespread and profound in our politics . . . , a current rearrangement of the past to fit and resemble the present, the obliteration of inconvenient history. . . . You can hear it expressed every day via our podiums and airwaves. It is the retooled "truth" of those who were always for "civil rights" or "always" against the war in Vietnam or "always" in precisely the position that today is generally deemed the right one.
>
> Strom Thurmond! How old do you have to be to remember where Senator Thurmond was before the passage of the voting

rights legislation (which he fought tooth and nail) enfranchised black voters in his state and caused him, expediently, to change his tune?

I look at senators and see volumes of history—of reality—that have been blotted out of their consciousness.

Great men—those who deserve to be remembered in history—are those who have served all the people they represented equally and fairly. Many of the civil rights movement's most prominent activists fit this description, though some did not.

I came into contact with a number of prominent civil rights leaders in addition to the King family—Whitney Young, Sam Williams, Julian Bond, Maynard Jackson, Sam Proctor, Andrew Young, Vincent Harding, Hosea Williams, and Jesse Hill. Although we had a common bond—the civil rights movement—I met them under varied circumstances.

One afternoon in the late 1950s I was attending a meeting called "Keep Our Schools Open" at the home of Eliza Paschall, a well-known white liberal. Whitney Young, who later became director of the National Urban League and was at the time head of the Atlanta chapter of the NAACP, had brought his two young daughters to the meeting so that they could play with Eliza's two children. The four girls, two black and two white, decided that they wanted an ice cream cone, so they headed for the corner drugstore on Ponce de Leon Avenue. The druggist told them, "I don't serve Negras." The children came back in tears. Eliza, who had traded with the druggist for years, promptly told him off. Then she sat down and wrote a short article about the incident and submitted it to the *Atlantic Monthly.* The *Atlantic* promptly sent her a check for $150 and published the piece in its next issue. I recalled this incident years later when I happened to buy some of the commemorative stamps that the post office issued honoring Whitney's memory.

I also remember the night when Dr. Sam Williams came before the school board to protest a ruling that he regarded as unfair to black students. Oby Brewer, Jr., the chairman, allowed Dr. Williams only a few minutes to state his case before cutting him off abruptly. Dr. Williams, who had not finished making his point, nevertheless continued to speak.

Chairman Brewer said, "If you continue, I will have you thrown out. The chair does not recognize you." The crowded audience, largely black, waited tensely. Dr. Williams kept speaking, and Chairman Brewer summoned the big, uniformed school guard, who happened to be black and who venerated Dr. Williams as much as most Americans do the president of the United States.

Afraid to disobey orders but clearly reluctant to act, the guard proceeded slowly down the center aisle toward Dr. Williams, who stood at the podium. To avert disaster, I quickly turned to Chairman Brewer and said, "I respectfully request that you allow Dr. Williams to finish." Perhaps sensing trouble, Brewer granted my request. Dr. Williams continued speaking, the audience relaxed, and the crisis passed.

Another time Dr. Williams and I sat together at a meeting of the National Council of Christians and Jews. A white Baptist preacher present got up and explained that this country had been founded by white, Anglo-Saxon Protestants and he meant to see that it stayed that way. He declared that integration of the races was against God's will.

The audience was stunned. Dr. Williams and I looked at each other and decided to take this preacher on. Dr. Williams's rebuttal was brilliant and to the point. I argued that our country had been founded to permit religious freedom and independence of thought and that its guiding principles had little to do with exclusive white Anglo-Saxon Protestants. The Baptist man of God was not willing to hear us, much less change his mind. He stalked out of the meeting when it had hardly begun.

Dr. Sam Williams was a philosophy professor at Atlanta University, a minister at the Friendship Baptist Church, and the chairman of the Atlanta Summit Leadership Conference, the most powerful civil rights organization in Atlanta.

Dr. King often described Dr. Williams as his mentor, "the best teacher I ever had." Speaking before a white audience shortly before his death, Dr. Williams said, "My one classic complaint against 'good people' is that they are good for nothing. If we could get rid of 'good people' we could change the world. So-called 'good people' do not take stands and therefore are in the way of progress. For once I'd like to see white people in groups protesting injustice."

Dr. King agreed with Dr. Williams that "good people" were good for nothing, but he expressed it differently: "Shallow understanding from people of good will is more frustrating than absolute misunderstanding from people of ill will. Lukewarm acceptance is much more bewildering than outright rejection." Dante, writing centuries earlier, made the point even more strongly: "The hottest spot in hell is reserved for those who never take sides."

Dr. Williams once said, "White America wants all Negroes to go the same way. It is too much to hope. Some will go down the violent road. Many young Negroes are reading history with a new type of eyeglass and see that the power structure rarely makes concessions without some type of disruption. Young Negroes, particularly militant ones, no longer believe what people say their intentions are. I want to believe but I am a minister."

Brilliant philosopher and theologian that he was, Dr. Williams told me in 1960 that in all his years at Atlanta University no one from the Emory University School of Theology, only seven miles away, had ever once contacted him. He had never been invited to attend a conference or to sit in on any meetings or discussions in his field.

What a high price Emory University—a Methodist college—paid for its prejudice and snobbery! Some ten years later, in about 1970, I heard that Emory had finally invited Dr. Williams to speak on its campus. As far as he was concerned, it was too little too late.

Julian Bond was another leader with whom I had contact. I met him one night at a meeting and was immediately impressed with his obvious intelligence, his beautifully modulated voice, and his skillful use of the English language. He seemed somehow to have received a good education despite the segregation of our schools. Puzzled, I asked him, "What Atlanta schools did you attend?"

He gave me a long, slow look, "I never went to an Atlanta public school in my life. I was educated in Quaker schools in Pennsylvania."

As a member of the League of Women Voters, I often observed the sessions of the state legislature from the visitor's gallery. Blacks also sat there in a segregated section. The members of Student Nonviolent Coordinating Committee (SNCC), of whom Julian Bond was one, soon decided that blacks had had enough of segregated seating at the state capitol.

I was there the day Julian and about twenty SNCC members defied the law by sitting in the "whites only" section. All twenty blacks, mostly college students, dressed dramatically, in the fashion of the day. They wore tan trench coats, dark glasses, white shirts, and black trousers. They carried tightly furled black umbrellas. SNCC members also wore something else that a close observer would not have missed— determined yet scared and vulnerable expressions.

I passed Julian and the group in the large marble foyer and called out, "Go get 'em, SNCC," and did they ever! Not many years passed before Julian became a member of the state legislature himself with his own reserved seat down front. Julian probably shared Malcolm X's opinion of white women's contribution to the movement. When I saw him at a campaign rally for mayoral candidate Andrew Young in summer 1981, he returned my greeting without enthusiasm.

Maynard Jackson, who attended the same campaign rally in 1981, greeted me with a broad smile and gave me a big bear hug. He was a lawyer from a highly respected, well-to-do Atlanta family and the former mayor of Atlanta. The two of us had known each other back when he was studying for a law degree. Maynard's aunt, Margaret Davis Bowen, was a good friend of mine. She used to say she had "worn out a lot of shoe leather" going door to door for me when I was running for office. She told me that Maynard, who had three small children, would bring his law books over to her house to study "out in the back yard where it was quiet." The day Margaret got word that Maynard had passed his bar exam, she called me. She was excited and joyful. All she could say was, "He passed, he passed, he passed." When I run into Maynard today he is gracious and kind enough to say to anyone listening, "This is Sara Mitchell, who was for us, and with us, when it counted."

When Andrew Young and his late wife, Jean, moved to Atlanta, Jean called me at Coretta King's suggestion. The Youngs wanted to enroll their children in the best public school possible and asked for my recommendation. After talking to Jean, Andrew got on the phone. We had met several times at meetings of the Southern Christian Leadership Conference.

Andrew said, "We have decided to buy a house on the edge of a white neighborhood because there are certain advantages. We think the school will be better academically, for one thing. Then, when our kids play with their schoolmates in the white section, they won't get lost. Everyone will know them and where they are by their color." We both laughed.

Jean and Andrew were delightful, friendly neighbors to have, no matter where in the world they went. Both were well liked in Atlanta by everyone who knew them. Andrew eventually became mayor of Atlanta. He also served as congressman from Georgia and became an ambassador to the United Nations.

Dr. Sam Proctor grew up in Atlanta and was a close boyhood friend of Martin Luther King. A former college professor, Dr. Proctor succeeded Adam Clayton Powell at New York's Abyssinian Baptist Church. Like Martin Luther King, Jr., Dr. Proctor was a spellbinding orator—intelligent, well read, and street wise. I recall hearing him speak at a black student rally. "Black Power, hell!" he shouted, "Green Power is where it's at and where it will stay. Get a good education, then get Green Power."

Once in the early 1960s Dr. Proctor told me how to act if I found myself seated next to a black person on a plane flight. "Don't say, 'I am glad to be seated next to you; I have always felt at home with blacks, etc., etc.' That kind of talk always makes me nervous. Say the same thing you would to a white person. Something natural like, 'I hope this plane takes off on time or I'll miss my connection. Then I can relax.'"

On another occasion he made me feel like a trusted colleague when he shared some troubling personal information about another activist in the movement. He clearly felt he was telling me something that would enable me to make a sounder decision in my work. When he had finished, he said, "I know that you will never misuse this information." I was careful ever afterward to do as he had asked.

Vincent Harding and I became friends when he arrived in Atlanta in the early 1960s to work at the Mennonite House. The house was a big, aging structure in a poor black section of town. The religious order of Mennonites had sent member volunteers to assist with the peaceful integration of the schools. Harding, a teacher and author as well as a community and civil rights worker, asked me to speak to the volunteers about our schools and the racial problems. Later, as I worked with Harding and the volunteer teachers, I came to know him well.

I recall going to see Harding's wife when his first child, a daughter, was born. I remember sitting in their bedroom and rocking the baby in my arms. Some years later, after Harding and his family had left Atlanta, I heard he had received a coveted grant to study the history of slavery at various libraries and archives in London. A few years after he returned to America, he won the Clarence Holte Prize, worth $10,000, for his book *There Is a River: The Black Struggle for Freedom in America.*

I remember Hosea Williams in connection with some ice water. Before I was elected to the school board I attended board meetings as an observer for the League of Women Voters. In the summer, before air conditioning, the meetings were held in a hot, stuffy, overcrowded room at City Hall. Miss Ida Jarrell, then superintendent, presided at the head of a highly polished mahogany conference table. On the table sat a big cut glass pitcher of ice water and tall glasses. As the long, boring meetings droned on and I saw the board members drink, my own throat became dryer and dryer, and I developed a mad thirst for that water.

After I became a member of the school board we moved into our own building across from City Hall. We now met around a semi-circular conference table. The cut glass pitcher and the glasses followed us to the new location. One night Hosea and a group of his young, noisy civil rights activists came to our meeting. They created such a disturbance that it became impossible to carry on our business. The chairman declared the meeting adjourned. The white members of the audience left, and the board members except for me filed quietly out of the room. I decided to stay and see what would happen next. With the controversial, bombastic Hosea, anything was possible.

Much to my surprise Hosea walked slowly up the aisle to the board table, picked up the cut glass pitcher, poured ice water into one of the tall glasses, and drank. "I've always wanted a drink of this water," he declared. How well I knew how he felt! Hosea had been a businessman before he joined the civil rights movement. He served as a member of the Atlanta City Council and later became a member of the DeKalb County Board of Commissioners.

Jesse Hill and his wife came to dinner at my house along with two other couples. Dorothy Yang, one of the other guests, told me years later that, when I was in the kitchen, she had gone to close the draperies on the big front picture window. "I don't like the way bare, blank windows look at night," she said. "As I was doing this, Jesse said, 'Dorothy, don't close those. Sara doesn't mind if her neighbors know she is having black people to dinner.'" Jesse Hill, a graduate of the University of Michigan, became president of the Atlanta Life Insurance Company. He was a tireless crusader for human rights and civil betterment and was greatly admired in the business community as well.

In the 1960s, the Atlanta Chamber of Commerce regularly invited the president of any company whose business grossed over a million dollars in one year to join their organization. Since the Russell Construction Company fit the criteria, Herman Russell received the invitation. He immediately accepted. The only problem was that Russell was black. The Chamber had never, in all its years, invited a black person to become a member. When Chamber officials saw the home address on his letter of acceptance, they realized their mistake. They promptly wrote another letter asking him to reconsider. He replied, "No, I've been invited, I've accepted, and I have already sent in my dues." For several days the spirited correspondence between Russell and the Chamber received front-page coverage in both Atlanta papers. Some years later Russell was elected president of the Atlanta Chamber of Commerce. I so admired Russell's spunk that I made a special point of meeting him. He was one of Atlanta's most successful and wealthy contractors and a generous contributor to charities.

Stokely Carmichael was seldom in Atlanta, and I did not know him personally. I heard him speak here only twice. He was a radical and a firebrand as a civil rights orator. I doubt that Carmichael was a friend of Dr. King's, although Stokely insisted that they were close.

"Dr. King was a great man," Carmichael remarked, "but his fatal error was that he made nonviolence a principle when it should have been a tactic. If nonviolence proves ineffective, then black Africans should pick up a gun, pick up a hand grenade, pick up anything, but get your liberation."

On this matter, however, Martin Luther King, Jr., never changed his mind. As late as 1966 he said, "I still believe in nonviolence, and nobody is going to turn me around on that point. If every Negro in the United States turns to violence, I am going to stand up and be the only voice to say that is wrong."

9

The Second Time Around

My second term on the Board of Education officially began in January 1966. I was now an "insider," but I would have felt just as alone as I had during my first term if it hadn't been for Horace Tate, a new member. Dr. Tate had been elected to fill the seat of Dr. Clement, recently deceased. Like Rufus Clement, Horace Tate was black and was a respected educator. In addition he was executive secretary of the black Georgia Association of Educators.

Fortunately, Dr. Tate and Dr. Clement had nothing else in common. Dr. Clement had been no liberal, and the black press had complained that he did less for his community than I. Dr. Clement—who had acknowledged being one of the men who don't like women who make decisions—had never seconded a motion of mine. Nor had he ever demanded that the board act rapidly to rectify a shameful situation in a black school.

Horace Tate was entirely different. He quickly became my political ally and personal friend. With his arrival, I had a colleague who would willingly second my motions and for whom I could return the favor. The psychological support was welcome. Now there were two of us even if we were still voted down time and time again.

Ann Woodward, a white woman, was a second new member on the board, but from the very beginning, I knew she would not side with me. Ann was polite and very low key in manner. She wasn't about to disagree with the conservative male majority. I don't recall that she dissented even once during my second term. She certainly never endorsed any of my ideas or suggestions.

Ann and I had disagreed in other arenas. During my presidency of the Atlanta League of Women Voters, we had made a study of the city's schools that criticized the schools' administration. Miss Ida Jarrell, the autocratic superintendent, at the time was a big proponent of the PTAs, and Ann was a PTA leader. Any attack on the superintendent was construed as an attack on the PTAs and thus on Ann.

The PTA communicated to me its disapproval by failing to invite me to any of its citywide meetings. The omission was particularly conspicuous because I had been president of my children's high school PTA. On one occasion I went anyway. Even though the presiding officer could clearly see me in the front row, I was the only official present who was not recognized. The PTA organization at that time was divided right down the middle between black members and white ones, and each group had separate (equal?) meetings.

As I've said, the Civil Rights Act of 1964 was quickly being implemented in our school system. There were more tough, integration-related decisions regarding school closings, the switching of schools from white to black as a result of white flight, and, concurrently, the issue of teacher assignment.

How many black teachers should be in white schools and vice versa? Issues relating to tenure and gender made the problem thornier. The board received a number of complaints from white teachers assigned to black schools. Most of the complaints focused on the new students' behavior. White teachers were surprised at how much the black students talked back and at how students would just get up and leave a class if they didn't like it or would not show up at all if they didn't like the teacher.

I don't recall that the board ever produced a formal policy providing for the assignment of teachers. As I have indicated, tenure, gender, retirement, and the closeness of the teacher's connections with the area superintendent—all of these factors were addressed on the day-to-day administrative level. We probably had guidelines that have slipped from my memory. I do remember that there were a few token black teachers in white schools, but I can't recall having heard any complaints from them or about them. Certainly there were problems associated with integration viewed from virtually every other angle.

As my second term on the board began, I wasn't considered any more of a "team player" than I had been during my first four years. My identity as a maverick became abundantly clear as a result of my involvement with the Education Committee of the Unitarian church. The chairman of the committee called to ask me to speak. I was glad to accept the invitation, since Eugene Pickett, the minister, had been very helpful and supportive during the integration of the schools.

After spending months analyzing both published and unpublished material from the school board and the administration, the Unitarians published their report, entitled *Better Schools: Atlanta.*

There is undeniable evidence that we have failed to provide equal education for black students. They attend larger classes with higher pupil-teacher ratio, they have fewer textbooks and library books, they have contact with fewer educational specialists, they have inadequate buildings and grounds, and less maintenance.

There must be a redistribution of all the tools of education. An equitable distribution of bricks and mortar is not enough. Even more important is an equitable distribution of teachers and teacher skills, enlightened administration, tailored curricula and effective integration.

This clear, concise criticism and the resultant publicity so angered school administrators and the board that they hired a detective to investigate the Unitarians' Education Committee. We assumed that they were searching for outside agitators or even Communists within its ranks.

Fortunately, when the *Atlanta Journal* learned of the investigation, it sprang to the committee's defense. In the February 3, 1969, edition, there appeared an article by Reese Cleghorn entitled "The Better Schools Report: Gaining Ground." The article stated: "We can see no conceivable justification for such use of publicly employed detectives. A parallel would be the use of the city police to investigate anyone who criticized the city government. Such a practice, whatever the precedent, is wholly intolerable." In conclusion the editorial asked how often detectives had been asked to investigate individual citizens who had criticized the school system.

Reese Cleghorn, a columnist for the *Atlanta Constitution,* also came to the committee's rescue. "Happily," he wrote, the committee's "membership was the kind that could stand the test. These are solid citizens. They had nothing to hide."

Members of the Board of Education blamed me for the Unitarians' report. Although I had not participated in writing it, most of the committee's members were friends of mine.

Once integration had finally begun, I still had plenty to say about Atlanta's schools. As adamant as I was that every child—no matter the color of his or her skin—should have the best educational experience we could possibly provide, I also believed that the board, the school administrators, and the PTAs were mistaken in their priorities on nonracial matters as well as racial ones.

In a speech that I gave in 1967 before the Atlanta Kiwanis Club, which was picked up by the press, I spoke of the broad range of my concerns.

Parents should unite—but not to have teas, bake and rummage sales, or to listen to the same platitudinous speeches year after year. They should unite against the sort of absenteeism that lets children stay out on the streets during school hours; against deficiencies in health and nutritional services; against the lack of physical training versus over-emphasis on team sports; against inadequate buildings and playgrounds. The PTAs should exist for the students' education and welfare, not for the aggrandizement, or accommodation of the school administration. I have been appalled to find out that in many schools the principal dominated the PTA programs, the selection of PTA officers, and even the spending of PTA funds.

I was also critical of school administrators:

The majority of professional educators have long regarded parents and the lay public with a certain disdain. School patrons today can interpret, understand and appreciate school problems. Ignoring criticism will not erase facts or failures—students who read below grade level and below their potential . . . , students who cannot spell and are not at home with numbers . . . , students who graduate, not only unprepared to do college work, but who lack the basic education necessary to enter today's technical-vocational schools. The administrators should remove all barriers to good teaching. Our tenure laws should be modified. There are thousands of good teachers, both black and white, yet because of strict tenure laws, the poor teachers are allowed to teach year after year, and the pupils suffer.

Even the news media came in for a share of the blame:

Before citizens can unite and fight for improved education, they must have an intelligent and accurate understanding of the present situation. But there is a seeming unimportance attached to education news—at least to coverage of the sort that would make it possible for the public to assess, evaluate and support good schools, fairly administered. It seems strange to me that teams of expert newspaper, radio and television reporters cover just about every local sporting event and that pages and pages of description and hours of air time are devoted to such events—while school meetings are usually covered inadequately, if at all, by reporters with little background in the field of education. The result is a badly uninformed and indifferent public.

As an insider, I could easily comment on the Board of Education. "I have probably said enough already, but I'll add that a school system needs a board made up of honest, inquiring, courageous, intelligent citizens—men and women who are not afraid to look facts in the face and demand change."

In response, the *Atlanta Journal* ran a lengthy editorial that read in part: "We hope Mrs. Mitchell's appeal is not just another cry in the wilderness. A large part of Atlanta's school population is being short-changed and the city will pay for this for many years to come."

As I continued to speak out against prejudice and complacency, I struggled at home with loneliness and self-doubt. My work kept me busy, but I sometimes felt discouraged, wondering whether I could ever feel satisfied that I had made a worthy contribution to humanity. On a more personal level, I asked myself whether dedicated service to humanity could replace the kind of love that can unite two people. Could a freethinking, independent woman with ambitions who dared to dream also be a good wife and mother?

There are still southerners who say, "I can't understand what is happening to 'our' Negroes. We have been so good to them. They have been so happy." Ray often said, "I don't know what has gotten into you—I've been good to you." Some southerners, especially men like Ray, will never understand. In some ways I identified with black people. As I struggled with my newfound solitude and independence, I was extra grateful for my seat on the Atlanta Board of Education, which kept me involved in the life of the city and allowed me to feel that I was useful and helpful to others.

In February 1967, I was invited to a dinner party at the Martin

Luther Kings', which I attended with about thirty other guests. I had a delightful evening. As busy as the Kings were, they found the time to entertain at home. Coretta was a gracious hostess and on this occasion took the time to introduce each of her guests separately, emphasizing the contribution that each was making to the civil rights movement. The Kings never served liquor, since Baptists frown on drinking. The guests, who were not necessarily devout, sat holding their idle hands in their laps before dinner.

The southern-style dinner of chicken, rice, a vegetable casserole, hot biscuits, and chocolate cake was served buffet style. The older Mrs. King helped make everyone feel at home. There was not the slightest pretense about the Kings or their home. Their house stood in a modest, working-class black neighborhood on a street lined with tall, leafy oaks.

After the birth of their fourth child, the Kings remodeled and enlarged their house. The wall between the living and dining room was removed to make one large room that could seat thirty or more guests comfortably. The living room floor was highly polished hardwood. Here and there African art—paintings, sculpture, masks, and small artifacts—lent an air of sophistication to the sparely furnished interior.

Coretta King was warm and accepting of my friendship. I confess that I didn't always live up to her faith. One morning she asked me to carry a picket sign in front of the Thompson-Boland-Lee Shoe Store, which was in the heart of downtown Atlanta. The store had refused to hire any black salespeople, although many blacks traded there. The Southern Christian Leadership Conference wanted white supporters to carry the picket signs from a belief that this switch in tactics would make a greater impact on the store's owners.

I told Coretta that I was not free to help. The truth is that I lacked the courage. The Thompsons were friends and neighbors of mine. They lived just up the street from the house that Ray and I had shared. Our children had gone to the same school. And their store was on the busiest block of Peachtree Street, so I felt sure that when I went to picket I'd see some of my friends.

I still feel the shame of my refusal. If Coretta ever held this incident against me—and I knew that she heard the hesitation in my voice—she never let on. She remained gracious and forgiving. All these years later, I still have a guilty conscience.

Of course, all the things going on in your life never fit into neat compartments—there is always overlap. So in July of 1965, right in the midst of my divorce turmoil and my second race for the school board, I got a call one night from Coretta Scott King, asking for my help.

Coretta and I had met on several different occasions during the early 1960s, but we did not become good friends until we both agreed to serve on a panel called "Rearing Children of Good Will" in 1964. Don McEvoy, the director of the national office of the National Council of Christians and Jews, had come south to work on behalf of the Council for "better race relations." He began this formidable task with a small first step. He invited representatives of the city's leading women's organizations to have lunch at a downtown hotel.

I came as a representative of the Atlanta school board. Other women represented PTAs, churches, and civic, garden, and women's clubs. Don asked the group, "What can influential people like you do to help ease the racial tension in Atlanta?" His objective was obviously to persuade white citizens to face increasing school integration with cooperation, understanding, and, if possible, compassion.

As a group we agreed on this plan: we would select a panel of five mothers to represent various ethnic groups in the city. We would ask the organizations present to invite this panel to their general meetings during the year. We agreed that the subject to be discussed would be "Raising Children of Good Will." The women selected to form the panel included Coretta Scott King (black mothers); Janet Rothschild (Jewish mothers); Eleanor Bockman (Catholic mothers); Dorothy

Yang (Asian mothers); and me (white Anglo-Saxon Protestant—albeit liberal—mothers). Since there was to be no debate, no fundamentalist, conservative mothers were included.

Several weeks after our first meeting, a preview performance was held at the downtown YWCA. The entire memberships of all the organizations were invited. A large, representative group attended. The reviews were favorable, and the panel was subsequently asked to appear many times during the next three years.

Panel members took turns telling how we had tried to raise our own children free from prejudice. Our approaches had included "not using slang or any slur word in referring to someone of another race . . . , not discriminating against anyone . . . , encouraging our sons and daughters to be as helpful as possible when someone of another race needed a friend . . . , speaking up when some racial wrong needed righting."

Our remarks were not prescribed or rehearsed, and so we never knew what the other panel members might say. We learned a lot from each other. For example, I recall that Shirley Jordan (Vernon Jordan's wife, who acted as a stand-in for Coretta when Coretta was unavailable) told us how she and her mother always walked instead of taking the bus when they went places together. "Mother told me years later that she couldn't bear having me ask her why we had to sit on the back of the bus. So we just walked."

Coretta and I became close friends during these years. After she got her children to bed she would often call me for a long chat, mostly to talk about our children, our community involvement, and our responsibilities as wives and mothers: nothing earthshaking.

One night in July 1965, Coretta called to ask for my help in connection with an important decision that she and Martin had made. Almost exactly a year earlier, on July 2, 1964, President Johnson had signed the Civil Rights Act, which in essence gave public school students the right to integrate all grades, thus doing away with Atlanta's ludicrous grade-a-year plan. Coretta said to me, "You know how long and hard Martin has worked for school integration. Now that we can enter two of the older children anywhere we want, we need some advice. Which white school do you think would be able to offer them the best education?"

I was pleased that she would ask me for such advice, and to be honest, I was a good choice. As I related earlier, when I was first elected to the board, I visited every one of Atlanta's public schools. Now, having served for nearly four years, I had even stronger opinions about which schools were "best," so I didn't hesitate long over my answer. I told Coretta, "I'm sure the children would be happy and get a good education at Spring Street School. I know the academic program is excellent, and the principal is fair and open minded."

I gave her the home phone number of Dr. Mark Huie. "He's the area superintendent and can make the necessary arrangements." About five minutes later my phone rang again. A clearly distressed Coretta said, "Dr. Huie told me Spring Street School was too crowded in some grades and that he could only enroll one of my children."

Any mother or father knows the frustration and the confusion that result from having your children in two separate schools. To complicate matters, Coretta added, "And I should have mentioned that Mrs. Ralph Abernathy [the wife of Dr. King's good friend and fellow civil rights leader] also wants to enter her two children."

"Don't worry," I told her. "I'll call you back in a few minutes." I knew Dr. Huie was going strictly by the school administration policy according to which any student could transfer if the prospective school was less crowded than the one that he or she was currently attending. I also knew that Atlanta didn't have a single black school that was less crowded than a white one, so I suspected some kind of ruse. I called Dr. Huie. "Mark, what's going on here? You must realize the significance of this request. I can just see the headlines now: 'King Children Refused Admission to White School.' I'm going to call Dr. Letson and get his permission for the King and Abernathy children to enter Spring Street School next week." I don't remember what, if any, defense

Dr. Huie tried to mount, but nothing was going to stop me from helping Coretta.

I hung up and immediately phoned Dr. Letson. By now it must have been close to 10:00 P.M. I explained the situation. Dr. Letson got the political picture immediately and said decisively, "Tell Mrs. King to have her children and Mrs. Abernathy's children at Spring Street on opening day."

I phoned Coretta back with assurance from the top that all the arrangements had been made.

On opening day, just as I had predicted, reporters, cameramen, and photographers from both local and national media were at the Spring Street School. That day headlines such as "King Children Enter White School" flashed around the world.

Coretta sent me the following letter. It was dated September 3, 1965:

Dear Sara,

Thank you so much for your help in making the arrangements for Marty, Yoki, and the Abernathy children to enter school this fall. They are all happily settled at Spring Street, and have gotten off to a peaceful and productive start. Let us hope that the peace and production continue! I feel sure that the children would want me to thank you for them, too. Your time and consideration are greatly appreciated by all of us.

Sincerely yours,
Coretta

Some time later Coretta called to tell me that she and Martin had attended a PTA meeting at Spring Street. "The program was on America's contribution to folk music," she told me. "There was no mention of any contribution the Negro race had made—no black composers, no songwriters, no spirituals, no musicians, nothing. I was furious." Then she, always the lady, caught herself. "I mean, Martin and

I were disappointed." Coretta has a master's degree in music from Antioch College, so she understood the magnitude of this insult to black musicians.

I also remember that a year or so later, an article in the *New Yorker* on the subject of folk music quoted Dr. King describing the same incident. Such a put-down—delivered by a school not only to you, the parent, but also to your children—would surely stay in memory, especially if you were leading the fight for racial equality.

10

Long Journey to a New Life

For me, the years from roughly 1954 through 1965 were a challenging and invigorating time with only a few major exceptions. The civil rights movement came to define my life in ways that I never would have dreamed possible. If I had not joined in the struggle to help blacks get what they should have had all along, I would definitely not be the person I am today. And ironically, the same liberal inclinations led me in time to a completely different life some 4,000 miles from Atlanta.

Over the past dozen years or more I had made many personal friends in the black community: Grace Hamilton, Sam Williams, Johnnie Yancey, and the ever-busy Coretta Scott King, to name a few. We continued to meet often for lunch, either at Paschal's or Herren's (one of the very first white integrated downtown restaurants).

Still, during 1966 I began to sense a subtle but definite shift in the movement. Nothing was said, and nothing outwardly changed among the black and white activists, but I began to feel less and less a part of the whole, less and less needed—or, later, even wanted—at the small backroom meetings, community events, and social gatherings where blacks decided their political affairs.

A day came when I had an epiphany, one of the defining moments that signaled an imminent shift in the course of my life. The occasion was a morning meeting in the large conference room at the back of Paschal's restaurant. I can vividly see the audience of about forty. There were fewer than half a dozen white faces. Up front was the speaker, Frances Pauley, a vigorous woman in her sixties whom I regarded as the ablest, most effective white civil rights activist in Georgia.

Frances was standing under the bright light on the podium stand. As I studied her white hair and pale complexion, I suddenly saw her as an outsider in a room filled with black listeners. I thought to myself, "It's time for a black person to speak and lead—not you, Frances." I was every bit as white and pale as Frances. Did the conference members still need me sitting there? In my moment of sudden insight, I doubted it.

By the middle of 1967, in addition to feeling less needed on the front lines of the integration struggle, I was also feeling frustrated in my work. I was at a standstill. Nothing I did appeared to make any difference. I needed a new direction, a different way of giving, of making a contribution that was positive and valuable.

In part the trouble was that I despaired of being able to change the attitudes of the majority of Atlantans. They seemed to me as prejudiced, as opposed to the integration of our schools, as they had ever been. The white educational establishment, the white churches, the white community at large—these people didn't seem to care about solutions. Indeed, very many seemed to be engaged in preventing solutions from being found.

It didn't help my overall attitude that I had been going around the country to one school conference after another. One week I was at the annual convention of the National School Board Association in Detroit. From there I went to a meeting on "Teacher Education and School Integration" in Dallas. The list went on and on.

I found most of these meetings a waste of time and taxpayers' money. School administrators totally controlled school board conventions and conferences, which invariably began with "orientation sessions" that taught new members "how to be a good board member." Newcomers were told essentially to "let the educators handle all educational problems and policy that comes up. . . . don't make waves, be a member of the team. . . . don't slow progress by asking questions." Conformists, we were given to understand, might someday become president of a school board or even president of the National School Board Association. Veterans who reached this point would presumably ask the school administrators to take charge of orienting the new board members, thereby ensuring that the cycle would begin all over again.

In the final year of my term in office, I wrote one more article that was published in the *Atlanta Journal and Constitution Magazine* on December 8, 1968. Its title was "Let's Face the Truth About Our Schools." I used much of the material that I had gathered for my speech to the Atlanta Kiwanis Club. This last important article created more tension with the school administration and the board than I was ever able to overcome. Once again, however, the public responded with letters of support and an appreciation for my willingness to face facts.

One letter writer disagreed with my criticism. His response:

Mrs. Mitchell condemns poor teaching, and so do I, but she does not define it. I have had students—both black and white—who would respond to no known methods that educators have devised. Some will do their homework and others will not. This has to do with human nature. The teacher is not a magician who, by some preternatural methods, cajoles the students into thinking.

The essential problem is one of good teachers and good learners. . . . For many years I have been teaching in different parts of the United States. I have taught seven years in Negro colleges. You appear to believe that inequalities can be removed by spending more money.

The writer helped me understand that it was one thing to crusade as I had been doing and quite another to be on the front lines of teaching.

I continued to attend some civil rights meetings but with a growing feeling that I did not belong there. One night I went to hear a debate between Stokely Carmichael, then head of SNCC, and my older friend, Sam Williams. The title was something like "The Civil Rights Movement Versus Black Power."

Carmichael was enormously entertaining, and the black college students responded enthusiastically. Williams, in contrast, was soft-spoken, calm, and reasonable, but he proved no match for his opponent's quick and fiery rebuttals. The audience clearly judged Carmichael the winner of the debate, though perhaps in that forum personal charisma, fiery oratory, and youthful good looks counted for more than maturity and intelligence. That night I sensed more strongly than ever that the civil rights movement had entered a new and disturbing phase.

Repudiation by those college students, the very ones he had helped liberate, must have been a bitter blow for Sam Williams, as it was for Dr. King and other older pioneers in the movement. I don't think that these men ever regained their spirit after the more volatile, younger activists became prominent as leaders. The older, calmer spokesmen continued their labors, but the work must have been harder to carry out in the face of such rebukes.

In fact, the black power philosophy that Carmichael and others espoused caused Dr. King much trouble and sorrow, especially because of its detrimental effect on young black activists. By the late 1960s the younger generation was obviously becoming impatient with Dr. King's insistence on nonviolence. On more than one occasion, I heard people denounce Dr. King as "De Lawd" who handed down pronouncements as if from above. I also recall him telling black militants, "You can't change my belief in brotherhood, no matter what you do or how you feel about white people."

By July 1967, too, something else had happened in my life. In April 1966, while I was in Washington attending a conference of the National Committee for the Support of Public Schools, I met Tom

Parsons, a delegate from California. He was introduced to me by the conference's executive director, and he asked whether he might call me when he reached Atlanta, where he would be working as a consultant to the schools.

Three weeks later Tom did call. We had dinner and a good talk. Our educational philosophies were in harmony. After dinner I drove him back to his hotel without expecting to see him again, but the next morning at nine o'clock sharp my phone rang, and we began an old-fashioned love affair. Tom was spirited, intelligent, attractive, and easy to talk to—and he was as liberal as I was! He was utterly, refreshingly different from Ray and the few southern men who had asked me out since my divorce.

Unfortunately, Tom lived in Arcata, California, a small town three hours north of San Francisco, almost on the Oregon border. It was a college town. Tom was director of the Center for Community Development at Humboldt State University. Although we were many miles apart, we talked by phone more and more often, attended several of the same educational conferences, and got together when he came to Atlanta as a consultant, which he began to do more and more frequently. In the fall of that year he asked me to come to Arcata and meet his two young children.

The relationship required me to look deep within myself. I was fifty-five. I had already raised three children and was in fact a grandmother. Tom was younger than I, lived more than 3,000 miles away, and was raising his two young children, of whom he had full custody. Where could I fit in this situation?

Tom was incredibly persistent. For my part, I adored being admired and appreciated for my mind and my beliefs. It was wonderful to have someone with whom I could honestly and openly talk about *anything.* For the first time I felt that I was truly loved for myself. The more Tom assured me that we would somehow overcome the obstacles that separated us, the more I wanted to believe him. As I appraised my own situation in Atlanta, I felt that I was standing at a crossroads. Eight months after we had begun dating, in December of 1967, Tom asked me to marry him.

I was by no means convinced that Tom and I could work everything out, but Tom believed that we could set a date sometime in the next twelve months. His biggest concern was taking me away from the Board of Education, of which he knew I was the most liberal white member. For my part, I felt that I had been fighting on the board for seven years with little success. In 1968, as my love for Tom grew and my misgivings about the school board and my work in the civil rights movement increased, I decided to listen to my heart.

When I married Tom, I knew I would be abandoning my southern roots. I would be leaving my mother, sisters, brothers, three children, and three grandchildren, cutting ties to many, many friends, both black and white, and walking out on my public service career. Still, I found myself coming to share Tom's conviction that what we had together was too important to throw away.

I accepted his marriage proposal, then had several serious bouts of cold feet, but Tom wouldn't let me back out. I could tell how strong his love for me was, and if it took his getting on a plane after a tearful conversation and flying all the way to Atlanta to persuade me again to marry him, that's what he did.

Of course, I had to carry on with the rest of my life during all my soul-searching. I continued to attend school board meetings, and I still went to some educational conferences. One of them is burned into my memory.

On April 4, 1968, I was in Dallas at the Adolphus Hotel for a meeting of black educators. I had been invited to chair one of the sessions because of my so-called liberal notion that all students should be educated equally. My topic was the problems faced by black teachers and white ones in integrated schools.

Having arrived several hours before the first meeting, I decided to walk over to Dealey Plaza to see the spot where President John F.

Kennedy had been assassinated. The Texas Book Depository loomed large, still dark and forbidding. Staring at it, I felt bitter and depressed. Returning to the hotel, I saw that the lobby was bright and noisy, filled with loud, friendly voices and faces I recognized from other similar gatherings. I quickly put my sad thoughts behind me.

Dr. Sam Proctor, now the senior minister of the Abyssinian Baptist Church in New York City, presided over the opening banquet. Dr. Proctor had grown up in Atlanta and delighted in telling stories about his boyhood friendship with Martin Luther King, Jr. Their friends had called Martin "Mike" in those days. It wasn't until later that Dr. King and his father both decided to change their names from Michael to Martin Luther, in honor of the great Protestant leader whom they greatly admired.

Since Dr. Proctor was well known as an excellent speaker and master of ceremonies, I was happy to see him at the podium. Following the ubiquitous lengthy invocation characteristic of conferences held in the South there were a few pleasantries before he introduced the guest speaker. I've long forgotten the subject and content of the speech, but I will never forget what happened during it.

First we saw a hotel clerk step discreetly from behind the stage curtain and whisper something in Dr. Proctor's ear. Dr. Proctor immediately stood and interrupted the speaker. The audience shifted uneasily and leaned forward, waiting for an explanation. Dr. Proctor then told us: "Dr. King has just been shot in Memphis, Tennessee. . . . there's no word yet on how seriously he has been wounded. We will keep you informed as soon as further news is received."

The audience shuddered. We struggled to go on with the program while people reeled with shock and disbelief. The speaker finished. Dr. Proctor, who had earlier left the room, returned to the podium and announced, "I have just been informed that Dr. King is dead. He was killed by an assassin's bullet on the balcony of a motel in Memphis, Tennessee."

In that large banquet hall, the Southern Conference of Black Educators reacted with stunned silence that gave way to low moans. People began slowly to leave the room in search of space that would let them grieve in their own ways.

Dr. Proctor came by my table and invited me to his suite to watch the news coverage on television. I accepted gratefully. As I entered his suite, I came on a scene I can never erase from my mind: first, eerie darkness, with the only light coming from a black and white television screen. Then in the shadows I began to make out the sad, defeated faces of some fifteen black men and women sitting straight, still, and silent. Unnoticed, I found a place to sit among them.

No one spoke. We sat mesmerized until the late, late newscast ended. Then we filed silently out of Dr. Proctor's suite. Back in my own room I couldn't sleep. When I saw Dr. Proctor the next morning, I asked him about the people who had seen the newscast with me the night before. Why did they not rage, curse, or show their anger? How could they seem so resigned, so accepting of Dr. King's terrible death? Here, after all, was a tragedy so great that it would change all of their lives.

Dr. Proctor answered me thoughtfully and patiently. "We've known since Dr. King's house was bombed in Montgomery during his early ministry there that he would be killed. What we didn't know was when, where, or how it would be done."

I began to understand. Insightful blacks had long been preparing themselves for Dr. King's death. It was like hearing that someone you love has terminal cancer. You grapple with the truth and begin preparing to accept it when you learn the news, not at the actual time of death.

The day after the assassination I flew home from Dallas. By that time the whole country was in an uproar. Everyone I knew was trying to get in touch with Dr. King's widow. Although Coretta and I were friends, I decided to stay away. I knew she had all the support she could use from her family and closest friends.

The next morning, however, my good intentions dissolved when I received a phone call from a friend in Chicago. His voice was urgent, pleading, "My wife and I HAVE to come to Atlanta. I went to More-house College with Martin. I know you know the Kings. Will you take us out to their house? We would be so grateful." I didn't have the heart to say no.

I picked them up at their hotel that afternoon, and we drove out to see Coretta. We walked up the high front steps and rang the doorbell. Coretta's sister came to the door. I introduced the Jacksons. Bill told her why he felt he had to come. The sister smiled understandingly but answered, "No, Coretta is finally getting some rest. Besides, everyone wants to see Coretta—all the way from the President of the United States to the ice cream man who comes by the house every afternoon."

We asked her to convey our love and sympathy to Coretta and the children and left.

On April 9, the night before the funeral, I attended the regular monthly meeting of the Board of Education. There was so much tension in the air, both among the members and in the audience, that we voted to adjourn after taking care of some urgent business. Even though civil rights activities in Atlanta had so far been admirably non-violent, the city was clearly tense. People waited and wondered, fearing some kind of rioting.

My fellow board members advised me to go home on the freeway. "By all means," they said, "do not go by way of downtown." I rejected their well-meaning but ominous warnings because I didn't believe that Atlanta's black leadership, or its black citizens, would contravene Dr. King's nonviolent principles. And I wanted to see for myself.

I drove out of the board's parking lot past the Fulton County Court-house and onto Whitehall Street, the heart of the downtown black business section. At 9:00 P.M. on this main artery through the city—Whitehall Street becomes Peachtree Street a few blocks north—there was not a single car or pedestrian in sight. A cold, blustery wind was sweeping down the street in front of cheap furniture and clothing stores, blowing the day's litter around.

At the deserted corner of Whitehall and Hunter the light turned red. As I waited I caught sight of the first human, a lone white policeman who stood against the side of a building. I guessed that he was there to provide protection and was trying to keep out of the cold wind. At his side was a police dog so large and fierce that the officer, a small young man, was having difficulty controlling him. The light changed and I drove on, but for a brief second his eyes met mine. He looked barely twenty-three and terrified. I reached my apartment safely, some nine miles further out Peachtree.

The next day I made no effort to attend any of the observances in Dr. King's honor. With so many national dignitaries, celebrities, and politicians clamoring for an invitation, I knew it would be futile to try to attend the funeral service at Ebenezer. I could have gone on the funeral march beforehand with the thousands of other mourners. I could have attended the ceremony that followed on the Atlanta University campus. I didn't. I was torn because I had previously made a date to meet with a group of white school employees. Also I worried about the huge crowds and the problem of parking. And I wondered whether I could get home in time to prepare dinner for the guests I had invited two weeks earlier.

Today these excuses seem flimsy, and I am filled with regret. Why do I always do what is planned and what is expected of me? I could have told my guests to come another night. I could have changed the date of my appointment with the school employees.

I did of course watch the funeral on television. I heard Mary Gurley, the soloist at Ebenezer, sing Dr. King's favorite spirituals with her glorious voice. I was glad so many millions of listeners were able to hear the music that had thrilled me on Sunday mornings at Ebenezer. That night, after my guests left, Judy Neiman called. She wanted to know what I thought of "all those people who were now praising Dr. King, yet would have nothing to do with him or the civil rights movement as late as one month ago."

"Many of these same people," she complained, "businessmen and politicians, have arrived in droves so they can be seen at his funeral."

I told Judy, "You and I know that the mourners who deserved

seats at Ebenezer for the funeral are not the ones who were sitting there—with a few exceptions, of course. Do you remember when the wealthy, social St. Phillips Episcopal Cathedral would not let Dr. King's children enroll at Lovett [a private school run by St. Phillips]? Well, today St. Phillips is holding a candlelight service in his honor. And I'm sure you saw in the paper today that Rich's [department store] closed today with full-page ads proclaiming sorrow over his death and high regard for him. Yet just a few years ago, every black in town boycotted Rich's because of the separate eating facilities and restrooms—and especially because of the blatant employment discrimination."

On the day of the funeral, Gordon Parks, a photographer and journalist for *Life Magazine,* wrote:

> Here were the ministers and his elders praying to God to take charge of the departed soul. And here was the widow, veiled and beautiful in grief. . . . in the coffin lay one who had filled us with a sense of hope that seemed, at this despairing moment, shattered. But in death he had made us know who we were and what we are.
>
> If the death of this great man does not unite us, we are committing ourselves to suicide. . . . to my black brothers I say, remember his words: "protest courageously, with dignity and Christian love. History will then say: There lived a great people . . . , a black people . . . who injected new meaning into the views of civilization. This is our challenge and overwhelming responsibility."

Dr. King said, "It is the quality, not the longevity, of one's life that is important." But I cannot help feeling that his death at thirty-nine robbed him of the pleasure of doing the things he enjoyed most: spending time with his wife and children, preaching, writing, and speaking out on the moral issues of the day. Death cut short his opportunity to be a loving husband and father to Coretta and their children and to be a comforting, supportive presence to his father, mother, brother, and sister.

Unfortunately, the civil rights movement had begun to fragment even before Dr. King's death. The national media, both in the South and in the North, had turned critical. Even his friends and admirers had begun telling him he was "failing in carrying out his goals." Youthful followers were giving up on his philosophy of nonviolence, of loving your enemies. They saw firsthand that nonviolence had failed in places like Cicero, Illinois, a middle-class, all-white enclave just outside Chicago. Dr. King's opposition to the war in Vietnam had also led President Johnson, the media, and many former supporters to turn against him.

As one of Dr. King's longtime friends told me:

During the last years of his life, Martin was surrounded with sycophants who, instead of helping ease his daily burdens, made his life even more frustrating. They argued about who would be seated on the platform next to whom. In Memphis, Martin's so-called friends debated loudly about what make and model car he should ride in. One said, "Mr. X will pick him up in his Oldsmobile," while another said, "No, Martin is too famous to be driven in an Olds—I'll get Mr. Y to come for him in his new Cadillac." They even argued over what kind of shoes a man of Dr. King's stature should wear, one insisting he should only wear alligator shoes!

What absurdity!

The year of Dr. King's death was a time of intense political and social unrest in America. The civil rights movement had spread outside the South to Washington, New Jersey, Michigan, and California. As long as Dr. King had appealed to America's conscience, pleaded for an end to discrimination in public accommodations, argued for improved educational opportunities for black children, and advocated full citizenship for blacks, people listened. When he began to address the hard problems of unemployment, unequal wages, the need to house the poor and homeless, and other issues relating to the need for equitable distribution of economic power, the majority of whites ceased to feel any sympathy for his cause.

There was a drastic shift in the movement after Dr. King's assassination. Restless, impatient new generations of blacks began to fill the void he had left. The Black Panthers and other militant groups became front-page news, while activities of the National Association for the Advancement of Colored People, the National Conference of Christians and Jews, the American Friends Service Committee, the Unitarians, the Human Relations Councils, and other liberal groups were pushed to back pages, if they were reported at all.

By 1968, the original nonviolent black leaders and white liberals were out. Young black and white radicals were in. Peaceful demonstrations were out. Confrontations were in. Promiscuous sex and drugs were in, and responsible love was out. And I was also out—or so I felt. White liberals were much less sought after or even wanted by the new militant black leaders. Of course we had long been out as far as white conservatives and moderates were concerned.

At about this time the *Atlanta Constitution* published an article about my activities that was accompanied by a picture. Someone sent me a copy on which had been scribbled the words: "You don't deserve your white skin, you are a disgrace to your race. Any white person who is a friend of 'niggers' should be killed." This was to be the last hate mail I ever received.

Now that the integration of public schools was well under way, and public accommodations were open to all by law, it seemed to be time for white liberals to reexamine their commitment. Letting go, after some ten years of daily involvement in the movement, proved hard, even impossible, for some. One person said to me, "Now that my black friends don't need me, I never hear from them—and after all I've done for them!"

With or without appreciation, the work of liberals became harder in the late 1960s. Much remained to be done in our school system. It was work that could keep us, especially me, busy for a long, long time, These were years of discouragement and despair for many of us but never hopelessness. Dr. King believed that if we kept struggling we could change things. He said, "If you can't fly, run, if you can't run, walk. If you can't walk, crawl, but by all means keep moving." Even in death he kept moving, inspiring us (when we listened) with his belief in nonviolence, with his unquestioning love for all mankind.

On December 18, 1968, I married Thomas Parsons at noon in the Unitarian-Universalist Church in Atlanta. The wedding was a small affair with just a few friends and family members. We decided that Tom's children were too young to fly across the country for the brief ceremony. That afternoon we began a long, leisurely car journey to California.

When we reached Yuma, Arizona, I sent a telegram officially resigning from the Atlanta Board of Education as of January 1, 1969. I didn't resign in person at a board meeting because I believed that my fellow members would be hard-pressed to come up with any true expressions of regret at my leaving—much less any heartfelt words of commendation. So I decided to spare us all. Fourteen days later I received a short, formal letter accepting my resignation.

For me, moving to the north coast of California was as strange and different as a move to Australia. I found myself surrounded by tall redwoods centuries old and by eucalyptus, not by the pines, oaks, hickories, and maples I knew. The soil was dark, not red like Georgia's. Streams and rivers flowed west, not east, and the Pacific Ocean always seemed to be on the wrong side of the highway. When I talked, people had a hard time understanding me.

But Tom was incredibly supportive, and I like a challenge, so I managed. Indeed, I flourished. The move was exactly the kind of soul- and mind-cleansing change I needed. Of course, I missed Atlanta and my family and friends, but we all stayed in touch. I grew up in an era where letter writing was a way of life, and my friends and I communicated frequently by mail. My own daughter Susan turned out to be one of the most entertaining of my pen pals.

Susan is my middle child. As with many mothers and daughters, we have always had a volatile, complicated relationship. Susan had no desire whatsoever to follow in my footsteps, yet in the 1960s she too was drawn to Ebenezer Baptist Church and, with her clear, ringing voice, became one of the very few white members of the Ebenezer choir. As a result she came to know the King family, but she was closest to A. D., the brother of Martin Luther King, Jr. He was outgoing, relaxed, funny, and in the lingo of the 1960s, "mellow."

Several of Susan's letters in 1969 kept me informed in the most personal way possible about the civil rights movement in Atlanta—and specifically about the King family. Susan was then in her early thirties, a divorced mother with three young sons. She had founded and was running a large, progressive daycare center and grammar school. In 1969 she wrote me in Arcata:

Dear Mama,

A. D. calls one day at school and says his car just broke down and if I am not busy will I take some Reverend (head of Operation Bread Basket) and him down to Zebulon, Ga. Lots of trouble and SCLC is wanting him to go down. I had read a bit about it in the paper. Seems the Board of Education in the county had let Mr. Glover, the black principal go when they consolidated the schools and put in a white principal instead. Mr. Glover had a #9 Certificate (?) and the white principal had a #3 or some such.

Anyway, a typical rancid move on the part of the whites in town. So down we go. Halfway there I notice there is a Georgia

State Patrol car following us. "A. D.," I said, "have you noticed that?" "Yes," he says, "they follow me everywhere." "How do they know what you are doing?" I say. "Tap the phone," he replies. Poor man, having delusions he is, I think. Four days later it comes out in the paper that the FBI, the GBI, and the State Patrol have a tap on his phone at work and at home.

Zebulon is 13 miles from sleepy Griffin [a town about forty miles south of Atlanta] and it is the size of the Emory University campus at best [Emory was then a small school in a quiet Atlanta neighborhood]. Heavy air, and the twilight as still as a stagnant pond. The black church is mud color. Inside lime colored crepe paper is on the piano for decoration; a picture of an impotent white Jesus is hanging from faded pink walls.

The Southern Christian Leadership Conference workers have been there for about a month. They are sharp, bright, don't take any shit, and are also quite beautiful looking, male and female. Beads and afros and a real to-hell-with-you attitude.

The meeting starts with a few songs. Lord God, can these people sing! A full church, ages ranging from two to 102 and they really are mad and ready for whatever comes. A. D. makes some meaningless remark (poor dear, he just ain't got it in that depart-ment) and the SCLC man from California strides up and raises the roof. "Go, you black fools," he says, "enough is enough. You will lose your jobs, be thrown out of the only grocery store in town, be spit at, but you had better get with it."

Looking over at a scene, get this one; little girl, neat and hair braided with love, holding her tired mama's hand. They are sing-ing, "My Mama is a Freedom Fighter and I am a Freedom Fighter Too."

So the march begins. Mist of rain in the air. The march is to take us to the jail where four SCLC people are in for rioting or some such garbage. About 330 blacks and yours truly. The white trash is waiting at the local filling station. It just seems to amuse them until they see your daughter and the comments come flying like bricks. . . . "white man's whore, are your babies black?" And some too much for your stomach, mom. The favorite was "white nigger." They followed us all the way with the state patrol lining the road. Confrontation to no avail. The sheriff is out (smart bastard).

We return to the church and the SCLC people say, "Does anyone have anything to say?" A few people get up and say they were scared, or they weren't. Kind of like group therapy and a brilliant idea after an emotional experience like that. I stand up and say that I have been called many names but never one so beautiful as "white nigger." I meant it, too.

The group decided to go back home and try again. The next Sunday Ralph Abernathy is in Atlanta so A. D. gets him to agree to go to Zebulon. Much attention over this in the press, on TV, and radio. After this buildup has taken place and more and more people in the surrounding communities, white and black, are interested. Even the black Georgia Education Association is planning to participate in the big march.

Now get this scene, about four o'clock on a hot Sunday: crowd meeting once again at the church, but this time there are, by AP and UPI accounts, 2,400 blacks and a handful of whites. Two white men are there and they both figure in my story. It has taken about three hours in the blistering heat for a march with this many people, to be organized.

Much gossiping, drinking of cokes, crying babies, tacky dresses sticking to black women, men looking the women over, especially me. One SCLC chick comes over and, with a big smile says, "Are you A. D.'s woman?" No embarrassment on her face, just a friendly question. "No," says I, "he is my pastor." She thought that was strange, I could tell. So hours go by and the group is finally ready. Ralph hasn't shown yet but no one seems anxious.

The march is to take us to several people's homes, or rather by them . . . , like the city's school board members. The town is so quiet you could have studied for exams in peace. White people are lining the streets yelling nasties and giving hand motions of a gross nature. The blacks are very quiet and suddenly they shout in union, "I may be black but [I am] somebody." A sound that truly chills the skin. How they all knew to say it at the same time I'll never figure out.

Now the patrol cops are edgy. The billy clubs are out and they are beating them against their legs. A. D. had asked me to march with him and the big shots but I got in the back of the line and found a cute teenager who had 18 stitches in her skull from some cop's club two weeks before. Two women and a man on either side was the arrangement.

Now get this . . . : the town doesn't know what the hell has happened. They have never seen this many people, much less blacks, assembled before, not even at the state fair in big, old Atlanta. Most of the men have a shotgun with them (I thought this was against the law). The white women looked like I have always thought the ladies of Rome looked when they fed the Christians to the lions. There must be something sexual in all of this. Anyway, the march takes us all around the small town. I am dressed in a new white linen dress, hair pulled back with a black ribbon, high heels, and Lord help me, a new panty girdle. I had decided that if I went, I would go looking as lady-like as possible.

In this second march even the State Patrol had charming things to say to me—like one walked right up three inches from my nose and spit out, "Why the hell don't you go home, white bitch?" One white woman came up and hit my back. I could have easily killed her but she was smart enough to know that we were supposed to be nonviolent.

We end up on the courthouse lawn and Ralph Abernathy appears. Do they keep him hidden until the last minute for fear of his being killed? The feeling in the air is one of impotence. What the hell can the whites do? The end is coming for them. The two biggest white men get an oil drum and some metal bar and begin to beat on the drum. The sound is almost deafening, making it impossible to hear Ralph. Ah, the townspeople are happy over this and they all rush to their cars and begin to blow their horns.

Pie-faced women looking on happily at the sudden brilliance of their men. Little white children riding piggyback on their fathers' shoulders shouting vile, stupid things. That got to me more than anything else. Suddenly a bit of violence as four whites knock over the reporter from WSB-TV and break his camera and his nose. The cops look away. It is just that simple, they look away. When the reporter goes over to one (and I heard this) the cop said, "You must have fallen down.'

So the march disbands and Zebulon is left with the biggest truth it will ever have to face. "Niggers" are not going to be "niggers" anymore. No matter what the price.

Some months later, in July of 1969, A. D. King was found drowned in his swimming pool. Susan wrote me after attending his funeral:

Dear Mama,

I have just gotten home from A. D.'s funeral and I feel as if my insides are securely wrapped in aluminum foil and are being stuck with straight pins. A. D. and I were friends. Not to get too damn dramatic but we knelt together holding hands in the dirty red soil around the jail in Zebulon. He said a prayer then for the souls of men hounding blacks the world over and I knew he meant it, meant his love. My throat is tight and feels coated with oil. Anyway, here is the funeral as best I can.

It was to begin at Ebenezer at 11:00, but you know black churches, nothing happens for at least an hour after that. I was in the choir. We sat for over an hour talking and laughing and then suddenly Coretta appeared, then Naomi (A. D.'s wife) and their five children. Perfect braids tied in fresh ribbon. Alveda, the oldest, a replica of her daddy. Skin the color of dried earth and in so much pain, so crushed that when she came in the door and saw the casket a moan so loud it was audible to everyone came out of her throat. That was the end of any laughter or talk. We got to the business of expressing our pain. There was no control.

Thank God. Control for what? These are the people who will go on. Not the Southern white women who keep themselves and everyone around them in bondage for years with their morbid guilt and mourning. Now was the time for grief and it began. Black nature (and I do believe in such a thing) gets it out then. No repressing tears and fighting feelings they KNOW have to be expressed.

The crowd was mostly outside the church. But inside we had several different groups within the black community. We had the old time church people, ladies dressed in their best pink hats and men in white ties. Then we had the clergy who had come from all over America to give support to their old friend Reverend King. Best of all were the young people, the SNCC and SCLC people. That is where A. D. spent most of his time. Two blocks away at the RIB Shack on Auburn Avenue and next door to SNCC. A. D. could have been almost anything and they would love him because he was Martin's brother. SCLC is the one black group that knows what Martin DID.

(The black militants can call Martin "Uncle" or "DE Lawd" if they wish, but we all remember when black children could not even go to the bathroom at Rich's Department Store, or ride the bus sitting where they pleased or, Oh Hell, you know. So let the militants shout and carry on. Martin was doing what needed to be done before anything else could be.)

The SNCC people came dressed in overalls, tee shirts with

black fists raised printed on the front. Bellbottom pants on the
women. The look on their faces said, you go ahead God, and take
any of us and still we will win—and they will.

The old members of Ebenezer were casting looks on the
SNCC members like my father would give "hippies." But these
people are where it's at. They live poor to help the poor. They
do not marry so they can travel and teach small communities to
unite. They are where I hope I would be if I had no family. And
all of them beautiful, earthy, with eyes that make contact everywhere they looked. I knew several of them from the Zebulon
marches and they are all college graduates, some from as far
away as UCLA.

First we all stood and sang, "Oh God Our Help in Ages Past."
A resounding vibration of good voices and strong emotion. Then
A. D.'s best friend got up and tried to read the passage from the
Bible about: If you have not love you are but sounding brass and
a tinkling cymbal but he just could not. He tried but the words
would not come. The audience, crowded, hot, overdressed with
not more than 10 whites, four of them ministers unknown to
me, were moved to tears with him. He looked down at Naomi
and said, "I tried." The church was one tear falling. He left by the
side door.

Then Ivan Allen [Atlanta's white Mayor] spoke. He must be a
good man, he told the truth . . . , that A. D. was overshadowed
by Martin but that if we judged him by fair standards we would
understand. Ivan was "feeling" without being a politician or pulling any crap. The audience obviously respects him.

Sitting in the choir it is easy to see the emotions. Once during
the funeral I actually saw all chests heave at one time.

Then Mrs. English sang, "There Is Something Within," A. D.'s
favorite spiritual. The verses tell of wanting the things of this
world, pleasures of the flesh, but there is something within that
leads me to Jesus. He fights me for my soul and try though I may,

his love and kindness wins me over. It is long, slow and beautiful. Anyone who had not broken down before, that included me, was at a loss. A. D's aunt from Louisville stood up during the song and looked Heavenward and said, "Take our baby, Jesus, Sweet Jesus, take our son."

I saw Daddy King reach over and take his wife's hand and squeeze it so hard the flesh turned white. Bunch never cried. She is a fantastic woman. I was crying so hard and had no Kleenex. What kind of fool would go to that funeral with no handkerchief? Several more people got up and talked about A. D. as if he were there, told stories about all the good and bad times in jails, and clearing up the rubbish from his church and home that were bombed, then sitting down to a good meal. One person even said, "No one could put away lima beans like A. D."

Then a woman so light colored I couldn't believe it got up and said she had come from Louisville to say something to Mrs. King. She looked Bunch right in the face and said, "Black woman, blessed is the fruit of thy womb." Her voice was so loud it surely carried downtown. The entire church stood as one with no signal given and said, "Amen." Then the choir sang, "It is Well With My Soul." Of all songs, my favorite: "It is well, it is well, with my soul." High and wailing, strong and true.

Then Reverend King got up and said he just wanted to thank everyone and he looked as if he was going to turn and walk away but he turned back to the pulpit and with both arms hugging himself he said, cried, moaned, prayed, "Both, O Lord, both of them gone." And that is when I saw the church, the entire church, give out a moan that surely penetrated the very walls and through the stained glass windows.

So they carried his body out. I yearned to talk to him again. On one of the marches he took off the heavy cross he always wore around his neck tied with simple black string and put it around my neck. He said, "I can't walk with you now and this will take care of you."

I prize Susan's letters greatly. I am proud to be the mother of someone who feels so deeply and who has the ability to express herself in such a compassionate, compelling way.

11

The Dove Flies On

Moving to California and living there happily, of course, did not mean that I abandoned my southern heritage. In fact, before I married Tom, I had gotten him to agree to a long-range plan: we would live for twenty years in California, until his retirement, and then we would move back to Atlanta. In the meantime I could hardly stay away from my family and friends for any extended period, so I returned to Atlanta at least once a year. In between these visits my friends sent me news clippings, articles, and programs from many civil rights events.

In California I once more became a full-time wife and mother and, once again, a volunteer for the causes I believed in. I joined the League of Women Voters, the Friends of the Library, and the National Association for the Advancement of Colored People.

Arcata was a liberal town whose inhabitants were 95 percent white. There were few burning civil rights issues to address. Still, even 3,000 miles from my civil rights roots, I had several memorable encounters, one of which involved Angela Davis, probably the most outspoken female firebrand of the early 1970s. In the late 1960s Angela had become notorious in California as a card-carrying member of the Communist Party and a professor at the University of California. An attractive woman with a large afro, Angela spoke out tirelessly and passionately against racism, poverty, and the Establishment.

When she learned of black prisoners' mistreatment at Soledad Prison, Angela befriended a number of the inmates. There was a riot and several inmates were put on trial. It turned out that Angela had lent guns to the brother of one of the inmates, although she described the guns as ones that she owned for her own protection. The brother smuggled one of the guns into the trial, and a shoot-out occurred. Two hostages were killed. Angela was indicted, went into hiding, and was caught by the FBI. She was brought back to California and served sixteen months in jail before being acquitted in 1972. She claimed that she had not been at the scene when the shoot-out occurred.

In 1977, I received a telephone call from a friend who was helping to arrange for the featured speaker at Humboldt State University's Women's Studies Week. The speaker, of course, was Angela Davis. My friend said, "Because she still receives death threats, we're concerned that Angela needs a 'safe house'—somewhere secret she can stay—and I wondered if you might help us out by having her at your house." "Oh, sure," I replied. "tell her she's welcome."

Angela spent two nights with us accompanied by her imposing black female bodyguard. During the day she was at the conference, but in the mornings after breakfast we all sat around the kitchen table talking and laughing. It turned out that Angela and I knew many of the same civil rights activists, particularly Julian Bond and his sister, Jane. Jane's husband, Howard Moore, was one of Angela's lawyers.

One morning, as Tom was combing his hair in the bathroom, Angela walked in and started picking out her afro. She acted as if this were the most natural thing in the world to do. Tom and I still laugh about it. We were glad that she felt comfortable with us. The whole visit was pleasant, and Angela and her bodyguard left without incident.

My association with Dr. King made me a kind of local celebrity. Not surprisingly, I was the only person in the small town of Arcata who had known him personally. After Dr. King's birthday had been declared a national holiday, I was often asked to speak about him at various public meetings.

One day an elementary school teacher called and said, "Mrs. Parsons, our students know that there is a new national holiday on the third Monday of January, but they don't really have any idea as to *why* they have it. Could you come explain it to them?" I immediately agreed—and then was dismayed to learn that I'd be speaking to grades one through eight—a gym full of fidgety kids—and she wanted me to talk for twenty minutes!

After wracking my brain, I decided to begin with a story I had heard Dr. King tell several times. It was a story that centered on his four children when they were young.

One time I came home from work and sat down to read the evening paper. My children—Marty, Bunny, Dexter, and Yoke— were watching TV in the next room, and I could hear one particularly loud commercial as soon as it came on. The announcer shouted, "Come to Funland!"—that was an Atlanta amusement park—"See the cowboys and cowgirls! Ride the rides! Eat popcorn, peanuts, and cotton candy! Bring your mom and dad! Join the fun!"

The next loud noises I heard were the children's feet as they came running toward me, their excited voices begging, "Take us to Funland, please, Daddy, please!"

I thought carefully before I answered, and then I said slowly, sadness creeping into my voice, "I'm sorry but I can't take you to Funland."

In unison, my children cried, "Why not, Daddy? Why can't you take us?"

At that point, I abruptly stopped the story and asked the students, "Why do you think Dr. King couldn't take his kids to Funland?"

Eager hands flew up all over the gym.

"Because it was too far to go," offered a boy in the third row.

"No," I said, "that wasn't the reason."

"Because it cost too much," offered another.

"Sorry, no. You in the blue jacket?"

"Because he was too busy to take them?"

"No, Dr. King always tried very hard to find time to be with his kids."

Although I knew virtually all of these youngsters had grown up in Arcata, I was worried. My approach didn't seem to be working. Had what my clever beginning to this speech been a bad idea? Was the whole concept of segregation totally foreign even to the eighth graders?

Then I noticed a small girl with pigtails, the only black child in the entire auditorium. I watched as she slowly but deliberately raised her hand. Without hesitating or mincing words she said, "They couldn't go because they were black."

I guess I should have been happy that all those white students knew nothing about the South's prejudice against blacks, but on the other hand, how could I make them understand something so ingrained in the South from the time a child is seven, eight, or even younger?

My experience on that day in Arcata taught me a lesson. Afterward, I told school audiences how Dr. King opposed *all* prejudice, whether it was against native Indians, Hispanics, Asians, or people of any different race, prejudice against people who don't dress, cut their hair, talk, or even think like others in the majority. After laying such groundwork, I could then tell the children how the black civil rights movement freed millions of people from legal discrimination enacted by whites, how the movement made whites take stock of their prejudices and see how wrong it is to judge a person just by the color of his or her skin. I told the students that most blacks had fought for their legal rights in a different way, not by physically hurting their oppressors, but by being strong in their beliefs, by being nonviolent, by in fact loving their enemies.

The teachers whose classes I spoke to often used my talks as a "learning experience." They asked the students to write essays, poems, or short articles about Martin Luther King, Jr. The younger students were told to write thank you notes to me. Some wrote:

"I didn't know that white people were not being good to black people."

"I thought the part where you told about Dr. King's children was sad."

"Back then it must have been most different for a man to stand up for blacks but still respect the whites."

"I am not going to give kids as much ribbing about themselves if they are different from me."

"I thought it was totally neat that you knew Martin Luther King."

"I think it was sad, I feel that white and black people should be equal."

"I don't feel that anybody is better than anyone else."

"I thought one interesting thing about your talk was how Dr. King died because I never knew how he died."

"I know I will remember him as long as I live."

"He was a great man, always thinking of freedom. He was a loving man, always loving black and white."

An eighth grader told me: "I have never been able to understand discrimination, having grown up with a sign on our family's door that says 'Peace to All Who Enter Here.'"

Adam Engleskirchen, then a seventh grader, wrote a beautiful poem, which he has given me permission to include here.

Martin Luther King
A dove of peace
he flew to his people.
His people in turn
provided a branch

on which he could roost.

Now he is gone.

But the dove flies on.

As I have said, I corresponded with my friends and family in Atlanta after the move to California. On February 18, 1972, I received a letter from Coretta King:

Dear Sara:

It was so good to hear from you! It was thoughtful of you to send the clippings and I am grateful to have them.

The kids are doing fine. Yoke is an honor roll student at Grady High, a senior, and looking forward to college. Marty, Dexter and Bunny all attend Galloway School here in Atlanta [a liberal private school] and are also doing fine in their studies. They are all still taking music lessons and are happy, outgoing children. As you probably know, I am quite proud of them.

Most of my time is spent in developing the Martin Luther King, Jr., Center for Social Change. The Center is progressing nicely and I am quite pleased. I am enclosing a brochure on the Center so that you can see how we are doing.

I don't know when I'll be in California but I would love to see you when I am next in the area. Usually I can spend only a minimum of time away because I feel so strongly that the kids need to have me home as much as possible.

My warmest regards and best wishes to you, and I hope to see you soon.

Sincerely yours,
Coretta

I next saw Coretta Scott King on one of my visits east, in 1980. She suggested I come by her office on Auburn Avenue around six o'clock one day the following week. She told me, "I'm anxious to show you the Martin Luther King Center—even though it's still incomplete. Afterwards we can go to my house and have dinner."

I tried to invite her out to dinner instead, but she said, "No, let's go to my house so we can really talk. The only child at home now is Dexter, and he's in and out."

When I reached her office, Coretta was meeting with the center's architect and the chief contractor. After they left, Coretta greeted me warmly and we left for the center, which was only a block away.

As soon as we got out of the car, five startled black women rushed up to Coretta. "We're in Atlanta from Cincinnati to visit Dr. King's gravesite. We never dreamed we'd be fortunate enough to see you— wait until we tell our friends back home!" Coretta was cordial and gracious, taking time to talk with them and signing autographs for each one.

The center, which I viewed from across the street, was a handsome complex of two well-designed red brick buildings. Running the length of the buildings was a long, cascading pool. I knew at once that this beautiful memorial would draw people of all nationalities for generations to come.

A guard unlocked the door and we stepped inside the empty, silent building. The foyer was spacious, light, and open to the outside courtyard. The inside walls and floor were red brick. Tall wall-to-wall windows looked out on the cascading pool. On the back terrace to the right stood an ancient, gnarled oak tree mercifully preserved by the builder. In the center of the pool Dr. King's marble tomb rested serenely. In death, as in life, he seemed somehow alone yet also a part of all that surrounded him.

Inside the building the floors were still littered with construction materials. Looking beyond them, I could sense the architectural beauty and functional integrity that would soon be the completed Center for Nonviolent Social Change. Coretta's vision, what she had dreamed of for twelve long years, had clearly become a reality.

We made a thorough tour of the empty buildings. Darkness had descended, but Coretta knew where each light switch was located. I saw the administration building, with its archives and library, conference rooms, and offices; "Freedom Hall," which has a large auditorium, a cafeteria for visitors, a shop to purchase memorabilia, and additional meeting rooms; and a room dedicated to the memory of Mahatma Gandhi.

Coretta knew every inch of the buildings as well as I knew my own house. While she was telling me about the structure, I found myself listening less to her words than to her way of speaking. I asked myself what had happened to this person I had known as the prototype of the southern minister's wife. The once shy and retiring minister's wife had all but disappeared. In her place stood a woman capable of raising the millions of dollars the center had cost, someone strong enough to withstand all the pettiness, frustration, and criticisms that had come from her own people, a crusader able to persevere year after year, just as her husband had done before his death.

While I was lost in my thoughts, Coretta talked on in a cheerful, relaxed manner. When she paused, I asked, "How was Martin smart enough, back when he was a just college student, to choose a wife like you? I can't think of another soul who could have accomplished so tremendous a task." Coretta smiled modestly before dismissing my compliment. As I looked around, I knew I was seeing a first-class complex of buildings as handsome as anything built anywhere in Atlanta. I was proud for Coretta and proud for Atlanta.

When our tour of the center was over, we drove out to Coretta's house. I remembered the modest houses on small lots and the pleasant, quiet neighborhood. We turned into the paved parking space in front. Coretta reached into her oversized pocketbook and finally found the door key.

I recalled the living room as it had looked when Martin was alive and I had been a guest at dinner. Nothing seemed to have changed with the passage of fifteen or more years.

We went into her kitchen. Coretta had "day help" who had prepared our meal and had set the table. She took our supper from the oven and got the salad and iced tea from the refrigerator.

While she was putting the food on the table, I looked at the family photographs that covered one wall of the kitchen. Clearly they were happy, private pictures. There were no covers from *Life, Time,* or *Newsweek,* no front-page newspaper articles—only snapshots. One picture showed Martin, smiling and well dressed, standing under a tree, with Coretta close by in a pretty, white summer dress. Their four children stood around them. There was also a picture of Coretta wearing a pale green satin dress before one of her musical concerts, one of Martin giving Coretta a big hug and kiss at the airport, one of the children at a family birthday party, and one of Daddy King and his wife, Bunch, smiling broadly at each other at a party celebrating their wedding anniversary.

Coretta said the blessing. Then we ate a familiar southern dinner of roast beef, rice, green beans and corn, and hot biscuits, with a fruit cobbler for dessert.

In the silent house, uninterrupted by the phone or any other distractions, we talked until nearly midnight. We spoke of our children and what had happened in their lives since we had last seen each other. Coretta told me of the many problems, disappointments, and frustrations she was experiencing in her work as well as the invaluable help she was receiving from various good-hearted, generous people.

Although Coretta knew of my divorce in 1966 and my remarriage in 1968, she had never heard the details. I told her that my husband had become increasingly upset, even angry, over my civil rights activities. We spoke of many things. As I was leaving, I turned and said, "Coretta, it must make you happy that the center is at last a reality." A look of sadness came into her eyes, "Sara, do you realize that thousands and thousands of dollars must be raised every year, year after year, to keep the center functioning? My responsibilities are never going to end."

Driving home, I thought about those of us who envy famous

people. We see only the glamorous side of their lives—the travel, the hobnobbing with other notables, the pictures on the cover of magazines, the interviews on national television. But who would really choose Coretta's life, with its pressure-filled days, the near absence of any private life, and the burdensome, always uncertain struggle to raise millions of dollars?

When I returned to Arcata I wrote Coretta, thanking her for her loving hospitality. Another twelve years flew by before I saw Coretta again. She was at an Atlanta book signing for Clayborne Carson, editor of *The Papers of Martin Luther King, Jr.,* and was kind enough to inscribe my copy with these words: "To Sara Mitchell Parsons—my dear friend and colleague in the struggle for freedom, justice. I am touched by your continued support and commitment. May God bless and keep you. Coretta Scott King."

12

What Has Happened to the Dream?

If Martin Luther King, Jr., were alive today, I wonder, as have millions of others, how he would feel about the dream he had in 1963? How pleased or how discouraged would he be? I think he would feel that the nonviolent struggle for freedom was more than justified—in fact, that on many fronts the battle had been won despite the remaining evidence of oppression, economic and social discrimination, and hate organizations like the Ku Klux Klan and the white supremacy councils.

Having grown up in the pre–civil rights days, I can see progress and change everywhere. Black children are going to better schools all over the South. They sit in class with white children. Children of both races are getting to know one another, learning to measure each other by criteria other than color or race. And yet it seems like the public hears only of confrontations, not the bonding of races. Black people sit down with whites daily. Personal friendships abound in the fields of education, entertainment, and sports, in the professions, in business, and in government service.

My country is not yet a sweet land of liberty of the sort envisioned by Dr. King, but the reasons are ones he could not have foreseen in 1963. Today our country is internally more torn than it was in the

1960s. Nuclear weapons are abundant, and the threat of war is ever present somewhere on the planet. We are beset by the problems of world hunger, environmental destruction, overpopulation, AIDS, crime, drugs, disease, and homelessness. True, some of these issues existed in King's day but not all. The world needs men of stature, integrity, and singleness of purpose to tackle these problems, just as King attacked the enslavement of his race.

America may be free, but millions of new immigrants cannot speak English, let alone sing "My Country 'Tis of Thee." God's children are now more than ever living in an unstable, frightening, ever-changing world.

Coretta Scott King has observed:

The dream is not yet fulfilled. But we are definitely getting there. There is no question about that. Martin said that economic justice would be the most difficult goal to achieve. He warned us that the privileged would not give up their privileges without a struggle.

One of my husband's dreams was totally realized. He promised our four children that "someday you can go to Funland." A reporter asked me, "did they go?" I answered him emphatically, "THEY DID."

John Lewis, one of the Freedom Riders and now a member of Congress, said:

If King were alive, he undoubtedly would still have a dream. He would dream of a time when the military establishment is free of racists, when the Ku Klux Klan could no longer operate with impunity.

He would dream that racial hatred in the hearts of Bostonians, New Yorkers, and Chicago's lily white suburbs would disappear.

He would dream these things and much more because the

dream of Martin Luther King was not confined to the Southland or even the nation. It was a universal dream of hope for oppressed people everywhere. If he were alive today, he would still dream the dream of freedom.

What has happened to Dr. King's dream? After a visit to Atlanta in the early 1980s, a reporter for the *Los Angeles Times* found the racial progress there "amazing. There is a degree of black power, pride, and participation unthinkable fifteen years ago. For many, black civil rights have been translated into substantial economic progress."

Gary Wills declared, "More than any single person [Dr. King] changed the way Americans lived with each other in the sixties. His power was real because it was not mere assertion—it was a persuasive yielding of private will through nonviolent advocacy."

What better way to assure that a person's life and all that he stood for is not forgotten than to declare a holiday in his honor? In 1970 the Georgia House passed an annual resolution declaring January 15 a day for honoring Dr. King. Almost from the day of his assassination, however, those who believed in his greatness sought to have his birthday declared a national holiday.

In February of 1976 a new drive in the U.S. Senate and Congress began in support of a national holiday. The two prime sponsors of the measure were U.S. Congressman Andrew Young and John Conyers, now a Democratic congressman from Michigan. The idea was controversial from its inception.

When the legislation finally came before the U.S. Senate and House of Representatives in 1983, there were emotional debates on both sides of the issue. Senator Jesse Helms, a Republican from North Carolina, launched a filibuster to block the legislation. "The legacy of Dr. King was really division—not love," he declared. Helms argued that the holiday would be a burden to the taxpayers. He estimated that it would cost from $4 billion to $12 billion to provide federal workers with an additional paid holiday.

Senator Edward Kennedy angrily contradicted Helms's statement. "Hogwash, that's hogwash," he maintained, adding that, contrary to Helms's charge, Dr. King had had no ties to Communists.

Robert Dole, then a Republican senator from Kansas, asked his colleagues, "Since when did a dollar sign take its place atop our moral code?" He suggested that those worrying about the holiday's cost "hurry back to their pocket calculators and estimate the cost of 300 years of slavery, followed by a century or more of economic, political and social exclusion and discrimination."

Senator Bill Bradley, a Democrat from New Jersey, in an extraordinary speech denounced Helms's tenacious use of Senate rules in seeking to block enactment of the holiday bill. "If only they had as much respect for the civil rights of all Americans as they have for Senate rules," Bradley declared. "King was a hero because a respect for democracy lay at the core of his tactics. Forty times he went to jail for his beliefs. He said he'd rather go thirsty than drink at the white-only fountains; he said he'd rather march in the streets to change democracy than be denied the right to vote in a democratic country."

The legislation was approved in the House by a vote of 338 to 90 on August 2, 1983. The vote in the Senate, held on October 19, 1983, was 78 to 22.

President Ronald Reagan signed the bill into law even though he had written a personal letter to former Governor Meldrin Thomson of New Hampshire only eighteen days earlier, stating that he had the "same reservations you have, but here the perception of too many people is based on an image, not reality."

A news cartoon at the time showed two letters, one from an "angry black American," which read:

Dear Mr. President,

I take exception to your remarks that the perception of Martin Luther King is "based on image and not reality." He took his battle for equality into the streets of angry Southern cities, pits of hatred and bigotry, preaching nothing but decency and nonviolence. He gave blacks courage and restored their sense of self-worth. For this he was roughed up, stoned, stabbed, thrown in jail, his house bombed and later he was shot to death. Image, Mr. President? What have you ever done to compare with that?

The other, an imaginary answer from the president, read: "Dear Angry black American, Obviously you never saw me in 'Hellcats of the Navy.' "

Despite the great strides in racial equality made under Dr. King's leadership of the civil rights movement, racism persists in the Old South of the 1990s and in other parts of America. The Ku Klux Klan to this day reminds us of how far we have yet to go. It is taking a long time for the South to live down its harsh treatment of blacks. Die-hard racists seem determined to keep the terrible legacy alive. In 1989, Klan members and white supremacists demonstrated their hatred of blacks by holding a march in Forsyth County, Georgia, and in Gainesville, Georgia.

The *Washington Post* on May 8, 1998, published an article by Juan Williams entitled "What If King Had Lived?" It read in part:

Had King lived, there might be fewer black politicians who lost their moral bearings. He served as a remarkable example to black leaders tempted by the trappings of power and wealth. Now there are few voices in the black community holding up visions of progress within the black community. On the contrary, the tacit message to young black people from the plethora of well-dressed athletes, movie stars and politicians who brag about their wealth, their political prowess and their development projects, [is that] a smart black person today is one who gets a good deal for himself. Talk of social responsibility is something for church folks.

In response to such criticism, I would ask, "Why should we expect the black race to be any different from the white one?"

Martin Luther King wrote, "One of the most agonizing problems within our human experience is that few, or any, of us live to see our hopes fulfilled." If Dr. King had lived, how different would our world be? We can only guess.

But the dove flies on. . . .

Index

Abernathy, Mrs. Ralph, 138, 139

Abernathy, Ralph, 157, 158, 159

Allen, Ivan, Jr., 88, 89, 161; and campaign for mayor, 40, 47, 48; and election as mayor, xii, xiii, 52; in runoff for mayor, 50

Atlanta Board of Education, 44, 58, 105, 115; and desegregation policy, 27, 31, 100; Dr. Sam Williams speaks before, 121–22; election to, xi, xii, 49; financial affairs of, 112, 113; and general experiences (first term), 73–79, 85–89, 111; and general experiences (second term), 129, 132, 134, 136, 149; resignation from, 154; running for seat on, 34, 35, 47; and visits to area schools as representative of, 82–83, 91, 109

Atlanta Constitution, xiii, 15, 28, 61, 64, 97, 153; and coverage of school board election, 46, 50; and Doris Lockerman, 65; editorials of, 56; and Ralph McGill, 10–11, 105; and Reese Cleghorn, 132; and reports on Martin Luther King, Jr., xxiii, xxiv

Atlanta Daily World, 33

Atlanta Journal, xiii, 15, 25, 61, 93, 132, 134

Atlanta Journal and Constitution, 87, 143

Atlanta Negro Voters League, 43

Atlanta University, 24, 60, 76, 78, 105, 122, 123, 150

Atlanta Voice, 70

Austin, J. Paul, 115

Bernie, Cassandra Maxwell, 24

Bockman, Eleanor, 136

Bond, Jane, 165

Bond, Julian, 121, 123, 124, 165

Borders, William, 15

Bowen, Hillard, 109

Bowen, Margaret Davis, 124, 125

Bradley, Bill, 177

Brewer, Oby, Jr., 122

Brown High School, 34

Brown v. Board of Education, 20, 28, 31, 51, 120

Bullard, Helen, xii, 37, 38, 40, 49, 117

Butler Elementary School, 83, 92

Capitol Avenue School, 59, 106

Carmichael, Stokely, 128, 144

Civil Rights Act of 1964, 130, 137

Cleghorn, Reese, 132

Clement, Rufus, 76, 77, 78, 79, 129

Cochran, Otis, 84, 85

Coles, Robert, 58

Connor, Bull, 80

Conyers, John, 176

Cook Elementary School, 83

Cook, Rodney, 114

Davis, Angela, 164, 165

Davis, Myrtle, 23

Dole, Robert, 177

Dombrowski, James A., xii

Durr, Virginia Foster, xii

Ebenezer Baptist Church, 42, 83, 99;
    A. D. King funeral at, 159, 161;
    and arrival of Martin Luther King,
    Jr., xxiii; choir at, 155; Martin
    Luther King, Jr., funeral at, 150,
    151; Sunday morning sermons at,
    92, 93, 95, 96

Emory University, 9, 123, 156

Engleskirchen, Adam, 168

Evans, Mr., 50, 51

First Presbyterian Church, 60

Freeman, Richard, 114

Gibson, Dorothy, 112

Gilette, Elizabeth, 39

Goldwater, Barry, 110

Gurley, Mary, 150

Hallinan, Paul J., 114

Hamilton, Grace, 23, 24, 141

Harding, Vincent, 107, 121, 125

Harper High School, 111

Harris, Roy, 118

Hartsfield, William B., xii, 37, 39, 104

Haugabrooks, Geneva, 42, 43

Helms, Jesse, 176

Henson, Curtis, 112

Hill, Jesse, 121, 127

Holmes-Jackson, Martha Ann, 34

Horton, Myles, xii

Huie, Mark, 138, 139

Humboldt State University, 145, 165

Humphrey, Hubert H., 69, 116

Jackson, Maynard, 121, 124, 125

Jarrell, Ida, 126, 130

Jenkins, Herbert T., xii

Johnson, Lynda Bird, 104

Johnson, Lyndon B., 100, 104, 110,
    116, 137, 152

Jordan, Shirley, 137

Jordan, Vernon, 137

Kemble, Fanny, 5

Kennedy, Edward, 177

Kennedy, John F., 32, 67, 100, 146–47

Key Elementary School, 85, 86

King, A. D., 98; and civil rights move-
    ment, 155, 156, 157, 158; funeral
    of, 159, 160, 161, 162

King, Alveda, 160

King, Bunch (Mrs. Martin Luther
    King, Sr.), 98, 99, 162, 172

King, Bunny, 166, 169

King, Christine, 98

King, Coretta Scott, xxv, 98, 125,
    140, 175; and death of A. D. King,
    160; and death of Martin Luther
    King, Jr., 148, 149, 152; friendship

with, 135, 136, 137, 141, 172, 173; and Martin Luther King, Jr., Center for Social Change, 169, 170, 171; and Spring Street School, 138, 139

King, Dexter, 166, 169, 170

King, Lonnie, 41

King, Martin Luther, Jr., 5, 57, 64, 97, 137, 171; and A. D. King, 155, 160, 161; arrival in Atlanta, xxxiii–xxiv; and birthday as national holiday, 165–67, 176–78; dream of, 174–76, 178–79; and Dr. Sam Proctor, 125; and Dr. Sam Williams, 123; death of, 147, 148, 152, 153, 154; family of, 98, 166; funeral of, 150, 151; home of, 135, 171, 172; and "Letter from Birmingham Jail," 93, 94; and Martin Luther King, Jr., Center for Social Change, 170; meetings with, xxiii, 91, 92; and Nobel Peace Prize, 93, 99, 113–15; poem about, 168–69; and Spring Street School, 137–40; and Sunday morning sermons, xxv, 95, 96; and younger activists, 144

King, Martin Luther, Sr., xxiii, xxv, 93, 98, 99, 162, 172

King, Marty, 139, 166, 169

King, Naomi, 160, 161

King, Yoke, 139, 166, 169

Kirkwood School, 104

Ku Klux Klan, xxv, 16, 32, 64, 65, 67, 174, 175, 178

League of Women Voters, xii, 18, 28, 34, 116, 124, 126, 164; debate over segregation within League, xiv, 21,

22, 23; debate over segregation in schools, 29–30; meetings of, 19, 20, 25; as president of, 27, 130; and role in school board election, 39, 41, 50

Letson, John, 32, 58, 74, 85, 86, 88, 107, 109, 138, 139

Lewis, John, 69, 175

Lockerman, Doris, 65

Long, Nat G., 16, 40, 68

MacIntyre, Dan, III, xiii, 38, 42, 45, 49, 50, 51, 52

Maddox, Lester, xii, xxv, 47, 48, 50, 52, 118

Malcolm X, 80, 124

Massell, Sam, 41, 50, 51, 114

Mays, Benjamin E., 95, 114

McEvoy, Don, 114, 136

McGill, Ralph, 10–11, 64, 105, 114

McLain, Roy, 55, 56

Miller, Samuel, 69

Montague, W. H., 89

Moore, Howard, 165

Morehouse College, 95, 98, 114, 149

Murphy, B. D. (Buck), 28

Murphy High School, 33

National Association for the Advancement of Colored People (NAACP), 56, 98, 108, 109, 121, 153, 164

National Urban League, 121

Neiman, Judy, 150

Nix-Beamen, Madelyn, 34

Northside High School, 33

Nunn, Sam, 118

Oglethorp Elementary School, 111

Paine College, 55
Paschall, Eliza, xii, 121
Patterson, Gene, 64
Pauley, Frances, xii, 111, 142
Peachtree Road Methodist Church,
    16, 18, 19, 54, 105
Pendergrast, Nan, 81
Pickett, Eugene, 58, 131
Powell, Adam Clayton, 125
Proctor, Sam, 121, 125, 147, 148

Ragsdale, Mrs. Clifford, 42, 49, 50
Reagan, Ronald, 177
Reed, Jerry, 35, 36
Richmond, Isaac, 70, 71
Rothschild, Jacob M., 114
Rothschild, Janet, 136
Russell, Herman, 128
Russell, Richard B., 27, 119, 120

Saint James Methodist Church, 56, 112
Sibley, John, 29
Sibley Commission, 29, 30, 31
Smith, Lillian, xii
Smith, "Muggsy," 48
Southern Christian Leadership Con-
    ference (SCLC), 125, 135, 155,
    156, 157, 160
Spelman College, 78, 105
Spring Street School, 102, 138, 139
Status of Women Commission, 18,
    19, 20

Student Nonviolent Coordinating
    Committee (SNCC), xiii, 124,
    144, 160, 161

Talmadge, Herman, 27, 111, 119
Tate, Horace, 129
Thomasville Elementary School, 83
Thomson, Meldrin, 177
Turner High School, 84

Vandiver, Ernest, 26, 28, 32, 80, 118
Van Hooften-Hoof, Mrs., 111

Wallace, George, 80, 118
Wallace, Henry, 15, 16
Ware Elementary School, 84
Waring, J. Waties, xii
Watters, Pat, 89
West Fulton High School, 109, 110
Wheat Street Baptist Church, 41,
    42, 47
Whiteford Elementary School, 83
Williams, Hosea, 121, 126, 127
Williams, Sam, 121, 122, 123, 141, 144
Woodward, Ann, 129, 130
WSB-TV, 49, 159

Yancey, Johnnie, 24, 141
Yang, Dorothy, 127, 136–37
Young, Andrew, 121, 125, 176
Young, Jean, 125
Young, Whitney, 121
Yungblut, John, 111